BEYOND CONSCIOUSNESS

WHAT HAPPENS AFTER DEATH

by Dr. Beverly Potter

Ronin Publishing, Inc.

Berkeley, California

Beyond Consciousness
What Happens After Death
Copyright 2008: Beverly A. Potter
ISBN: 978-1-57951-083-1

Published by
Ronin Publishing, Inc.
PO Box 22900
Oakland, CA 94609
www.roninpub.com

Cover art: Paul Heussenstamm   *www.mandalas.com*

Fonts:

Abad - Monotype; Ale and Wenches - Nate Piekos; Baker Signet - Adobe; Blackbeard - Ethan Dunham; Bodoni - Adobe; Bookman Old Style - Monotype; Braveworld - Ethan Dunham; Burton's Nightmare - Digital Type; Century School - Monoype; Chisel - Elsner + Flake; Dry Cowboy - Chank; Fiorne - Weatherly Systems; Fornicator - Chank; Holsteim - Ethan Dunham; Kingdom - Ethan Dunham; Mob Concrete - Ray Larabie; Morpheus - Kiwi Media; Orbital - Chank; Park Avenue - Adobe; Skia - Apple; Swister - Chank; Twylite Zone - Oliver Cone; Univers - Adobe; Valdemar - Scriptorium; Zsazsa - Chank.

Copyright Info: Expert quotes reprinted are from Works in the public domain or used under the "doctrine of fair use", Sec. 107 of the Copyright Law. Specific permission to reprint: From *Conversations with God: An Uncommon Dialogue, Bk 1* by Neale Donald Walsch, (c) 1995 by Neale Donald Walsch. Used by permission of G. P. Putman's Sons; From *Reading the Enemy's Mind* by Paul H. Smith, (c) 2004. Used by permission of Forge Books; From *We Live Forever: The Real Truth About Death,* (c) 2004, by P.M.H. Atwater, ARE Press; From Jeffrey Mishlove, Fred Alan Wolf, Paul von Ward, Stephen A. Schwartz, PMH Atwater, Rory Goff, and Gary Schwartz.

Library of Congress Card Number: 2008931384
Distributed to the book trade by **PGW/Perseus**
Printed in the United States by **Delta/Bang**

Beyond Consciousness

What Happens After Death

by Dr. Beverly Potter

About The Author

Dr. Beverly Potter received her doctorate in counseling psychology from Stanford University and her masters in vocational rehabilitation counseling from San Francisco State University.

Beverly's work blends philosophies of humanistic psychology, social learning theory and Eastern philosophies. She is best known for her original work on how to overcome job burnout and how to soothe worrywarting.

Her website is docpotter.com. Please visit.

ACKNOWLEDGEMENT

Appreciation is extended to the experts and thinkers whose wise words are quoted herein, many of whom are already on the other side and, if only we could receive their messages, could tell us much about the mysterious transiion we call "death".

A special thanks to Jeffrey Mishlove, host of the Thinking Allowed TV series and founder of Inpresence Intuition Network and to Inpresence members PMH Atwater, Echo Bodine, Lyn Buchanan, Stephen Schwartz, Paul H. Smith, Paul von Ward, and Fred Alan Wolf—Dr. Quantum, for their inspiring works and generosity. I am also grateful to Rosemary Altea, George Anderson, Rory Goff, Bill and Judy Guggenheim, Lori Lothian, Char Margolis, Raymond Moody, Timothy Owe, Elizabeth Kubler-Ross, James von Praagh, Neale Donald Walsch, Brian Weiss, Carla Wills-Brandon, and Gary Zukav for their informative works.

Finally, I am grateful to you, Dear Reader, who have taken the time to read this little book. May you be soothed and inspired by the thoughts and wisdom of the expects quoted. As John C. Lilly said, "We shall meet somewhere in alternity."

TABLE OF CONTENTS

Death is life's greatest event.

—Timothy Leary

INTRODUCTION

For thousands of years, we mortals have sought an answer to the question: what happens when we die? Death is the ultimate human enigma. Some religious texts describe an afterlife that is a reward for those who are pure in heart and repentant for their sins. Some describe reincarnation and past lives—a process of continual rebirth on Earth for the purpose of learning new lessons. Many people believe that upon the moment of death, everything simply fades to a black, quiet darkness as our memories and consciousness cease to exist.

What happens when we die? is one of the great questions of life. Is death the end of human existence and consciousness? Or do we continue in some other place or state of being? Do we go to a place of everlasting reward or eternal torment? Are we destined to be reincarnated, coming to life again in a different body in a seemingly endless cycle of living and dying? Will we ever be with deceased loved ones again? Is there somewhere we can go to find the answers?

At one time or another we all wonder what happens after death. We know that the body becomes useless and quickly decays. But what of consciousness? What happens to our awareness? To our souls? Do we have a soul?

It appears to me impossible that I should cease to exist, or that this active, restless spirit, equally alive to joy and sorrow, should be only organized dust——ready to fly abroad the moment the spring snaps, or the spark goes out, which kept it together. Surely something resides in this heart that is not perishable——and life is more than a dream.

——Mary Wollstonecraft

Thinking about death brings up so many questions. Is this life all there is? Is it true that when we die, that's it—no more us? Or do we live on after death, continuing to experience things in new realms? Does consciousness continue after we die? Are we immortal souls? Is there an afterlife of reward or punishment? What can we expect to happen when we die?

As conscious beings, do we possess spirits and souls? Are we sparks of the divine fire? How close are we to understanding the origins of the universe, of life, of consciousness? Is it possible to answer questions such as .... Who are we? What does it mean to be human? What is the ultimate nature of matter? Of mind?

—Jeffrey Mishlove
Roots of Consciousness

All difficult questions. Atheists and theists will answer on opposite sides of the matter. Most western atheists don't believe in any sort of soul or afterlife, while most theists believe in some sort of soul and afterlife.

Religious explanations offer a variety of answers, which are often contradictory and incredible, adding to the confusion and uncertainty about what happens after death. Some reassure us that we have immortal souls, which survive death. Some tell us that after death our soul proceeds to an afterlife of bliss or torment; others teach that upon death our soul returned to the Godhead; still others promise that we will reincarnate to be reborn as another person or even as an animal.

Is the human being merely an advanced biological machine, built by atoms to perpetuate genes and perhaps to service as a host for bacteria; or are human bodies physical containers of a spirit that lives on beyond these bodies inevitable demise?

—Timothy Owe
Beyond Death

In spite of centuries of research, science cannot tell us when, where or how life began. Scriptures and religious bibles purport to tell us how life began and for what purpose. Shouldn't we go to these sources to understand the mystery of death? What about people who have had a near-death experience (NDE)? These are people who have been declared dead—clinically—and then somehow returned to life. Their remarkably similar experiences offer a fascinating view of death. Along this same line of inquiry are the data from remote viewing, hypnotic regressions, after-death communication (ADE), and clairvoyance.

To fear death, gentlemen, is nothing other than to think oneself wise when one is not; for it is to think one knows what one does not know. No man knows whether death may not even turn out to be the greater of blessings for a human being, and yet people fear it as if they knew for certain that it is the greatest of evils.

—Socrates
Just before drinking the hemlock

I think, therefore I am.
—Rene Descartes

1

CONSCIOUSNESS

Consciousness is paradoxical. We all have it and we all know what it is, but scientists and philosophers cannot agree upon what it is or even if it actually exists at all.

Everything that we think of as "real" in scientific terms has a physical form that can be perceived by our senses. But this model, which philosophers call "radical materialism," cannot explain the existence of consciousness because consciousness has no physical essence. Scientists do not have a problem studying the physical brain. They can cut open the skull and find a physical brain. The mind, on the other hand, presents a mired of problems for scientific examination because it cannot be found. Where is the mind? Is it in the brain? Or does it reside in all of the cells and organs?

Philosophers have another theory to deal with this paradox, called the "transcendent" view that proposes that the basic building block of the universe is not physical matter but consciousness itself. This perspective is shared by many followers of the world's religions.

We turn to science to help us understand our world. We know what a tornado is, for example, because science has studied and explained them. Science knows a lot about the brain and how it works, but how the mind works remains a mystery. Science can describe nerve cells and the transmission of impulses across the synapses. But science is mystified when it comes to understanding the mechanism for how the brain generates thoughts or how consciousness comes about. Science has not been able to generate a single thought from brain cells in the laboratory. Yet, we all have thoughts. The concept of a soul helps to explain thinking and consciousness, but science doesn't recognize the existence of a soul. If the soul cannot be found, how can it be studied? So science either denies that souls exist or simply ignores the question altogether.

Science has a hard time acknowledging the existence of consciousness and defining it.

Consciousness is the ability to perceive the relationship between oneself and one's environment. It is described with qualities such as subjectivity, self-awareness, sapience, and sentience. In common parlance, consciousness denotes being awake and responsive to one's environment; this contrasts with being asleep or in a coma. Consciousness is characterized by sensation, emotion, volition, thought, and awareness.

Consciousness is that which facilitates awareness. Consciousness is not the same as spirit or soul, but rather the process by which spirit or soul creates or retains awareness.

—Timothy Owe
Beyond Death

Some philosophers divide consciousness into phenomenal consciousness, which is subjective experience itself, and access consciousness, which refers to the universal availability of information to processing systems in the brain. Simply stated, phenomenal consciousness is being something and access consciousness is being aware of something.

Consciousness is the mental function through which people experience things. This kind of functioning has some significant characteristics. Some states of consciousness, such as sleeping and dreaming occur naturally in the individual's daily experience. Others, such as meditation, channeling and hypnosis, occur in a particular situation, while others can be produced by certain drugs such as alcohol or marijuana.

First person experiences are the essentially subjective, personal feelings or experiences that each of us have, such as the feeling of being too warm or being afraid, and that cannot be fully described by words, formulas, programs or any other objective representation.

The first concept associated with consciousness is "awareness". We are conscious when we are aware. This is immediately seen to be not quite true. We may be aware, for instance, without really being conscious of being aware. Awareness is, therefore, only a part of consciousness. Other known aspects of consciousness are free will, reasoning, visual imagery, recalling and making choices.

Philosophers tell us that what raises humans above other known sentient beings is our ability to be conscious of our own consciousness.

"Why am I me?" The chills and sensations of first being conscious of myself being conscious of myself are still vivid in my memory. I was a ten-year-old child then, sitting alone in my parents' bedroom, touching my own solid consciousness and wondering at it. I was stepping through the looking glass seeing myself being myself seeing myself being myself...tasting infinity in a small body.

I could be anybody. But I happen to be me. Why not someone else? And if I were someone else, could I not still be me? What does it mean to be an individual being? How is it possible that I exist? How is it I am able to sense myself? What is the self I sense I am? How is it I am able to be conscious? What does it mean to exercise consciousness?

—Jeffrey Mishlove
Roots of Consciousness

Jeffrey Mishlove is not the first philosopher to contemplate consciousness and wonder how he could be himself and what it all means. What we are, how we came to be, and what happens to us—to me—after death is a mystery that has fascinated and worried philosophers and just plain folk for as long as we've been around.

One of life's greatest mysteries is what happens after death. Many religions promise that if we live a moral life we will have a wonderful afterlife. Skeptics and atheists reject this promise, saying that when you're dead, you're dead and that's that! The body, once vibrant and active, sensitive and aware, is inert, without sensation at death. How can there be any afterlife when the body dies and rots? What does it mean to be alive without a body?

Life after death becomes more plausible when we shift our notion of the afterlife from being a place to being a state of awareness. We must take care to not be distracted from the important questions by arguing over religious beliefs. Central to this query is the question: Is the mind outside the brain? Can consciousness (whatever it actually is!) exist outside of and separate from the brain? If it can—and there is evidence that it can—then it is plausible that consciousness—awareness, beingness, I-ness—continues after death of the physical body. Just as we can drive a car and then get out and leave it on the side of the road, so too, perhaps the soul can occupy a body and then leave it aside at death—possibly to be reborn into a new body.

In modern culture the idea that our consciousness survives death is sort of strange and maybe even a little spooky, scary to people. At one time this was considered simply the way it was.

—Willis Harman
Interview by Jeffrey Mishlove
Thinking Allowed

We tend to equate consciousness with the process of thinking. Instruments can record electrical impulses in the brain when thinking, but these recordings are not "thoughts". Thoughts are not constrained to the brain.

In the province of the mind what one believes to be true, either is true or becomes true within certain limits. These limits are to be found experimentally and experientially. When so found these limits turn out to be further beliefs to be transcended. In the province of the mind there are no limits. However, in the province of the body there are definite limits not to be transcended.

—John C. Lilly, M.D.
The Quiet Center

As we shall explore later in this book, science has confirmed that consciousness can reach out across the globe to "view" distant locations. Thoughts can have a physical impact on things and persons separate from oneself.

Around the world thoughts shall fly in the twinkling of an eye.
—Nostradamus

There is no argument that the body ceases to function and decays after death. It is just a big lump of tissue. It cannot move. Within a few hours it begins decaying and giving off a horrible odor. Where did the person who occupied that body go? We all wonder about this when faced with the death of a relative or beloved pet. How could they be so alive and vibrant one minute and completely gone the next? Where are they now? How could this bigger-than-life person or this wonderful loving doggie just evaporate? Poof—gone! We call it "passing away". Passing away to where? Why? Where were we before waking up in this body? It is hard to comprehend, much else to accept.

Do Not Go Gentle
Into That Good Night

D o not go gentle into that good night,
Old age should burn and rave at close of day;
Rage, rage against the dying of the light.
Though wise men at their end know dark is right,
Because their words had forked no lightning they
Do not go gentle into that good night.

—Dylan Thomas

But accept death as "the end" we must
—or must we?

Obviously we cannot really know what happens after death until we each die . . . and that is not a very comforting thought. I am the center of my universe and you are the center of your universe.

I have a body and I am more than my body.
I have emotions and I am more than my emotions.

I have a mind and I am more than my mind.
I am a center of pure consciousness and energy.

—*The New Living Kabala*

What happens to my universe and your universe when we die? What do scientists, philosophers and theists have to say? We can collect clues about what happens to consciousness after death—if indeed consciousness does survive. If consciousness does survive death, is it possible to experience such disembodied consciousness without dying?

As we shall see later in this book, many people have had "near-death experiences" or NDEs, where they were declared clinically dead and then were revived. Many people to whom this has happened report a world of awareness while they were "dead" and reports of their experiences while dead are remarkably similar. Is this evidence of an afterlife? When these people where nearly dead—but not really dead since they came back to life—were they actually in the afterlife and experiencing it? Many say, "yes!" Reports from people who have had NDEs offer hope and provide clues as to what happens after death.

Science has avoided studying consciousness and the existence of an afterlife partly because science has not asked the right questions. While we all have plenty of questions about death and afterlife, crafting questions for empirical investigation continues to allude scientists.

Does conscious awareness naturally emerge from the complex structure of physical atoms, molecules, cells and organs that compose my body? Does consciousness reside somehow or emerge from the higher structure of my brain and nervous system? And, if so, how does that occur? What is it about the structure of my nervous system that allows me to discover myself as a human being? How can a brain formulate questions? Are thoughts and questions even things in the same sense that neurons and brains are things?

—Jeffrey Mishlove
Roots of Consciousness

Curious, isn't it? Science can tell us the composition of the gases in the rings around Saturn, which is millions of light years away where no human has visited, yet science can tell us so little about that which is closest to us—our minds, our consciousness, our beingness.

We need to do much larger studies, but the possibility is certainly here to suggest that consciousness, or the soul, keeps thinking and reasoning even when a person's heart has stopped, he or she is not breathing, and brain activity is nil.

—Sam Parnia

Science can put robots on Mars. Science can create artificial hearts and put them into humans who live on with the mechanical device. Science can create fabulous flat screen TVs and the internet with all of its amazing features. But science can tell us very little about what happens after death. Until science recognizes the validity of such inquiry, we must turn to philosophers and theist and psychologists for answers, or at least for clues as to what will happen.

Life and subsequent death with its release of consciousness is merely part of an ongoing process: the development of consciousness, or spirit, within and without the body.

—Timothy Owe
Beyond Death

WHat is consciousness?

Consciousness is a singular of which the plural is unknown. There is only one thing, and that which seems to be plurality is merely a series of different aspects of this one thing, produced by a deception, the Indian *maya*, as in a gallery of mirrors.

—Erwin Schrodinger
Nobel Physicist

Of course we know what consciousness is—until we try to describe it. Then, like the seven sages, we discover that we each have a different definition. What we do know is that consciousness is more than a "brain" function.

Beyond the Seven States of Consciousness

Seven Sages were arguing over the ultimate shape of Reality, or Consciousness.

"Reality is a point!" said the first. "The foundation of existence is the timeless nothingness of Deep Sleep!"

"No, Reality is a line!" said the second. "Life is Consciousness moving as Thought; Life is but a Dream!"

"No, no; you're both wrong! Reality is a plane: two lines intersecting in an X!" said the third. "Truly, Waking State is the most logical of Realities!"

"Oh, you poor blind fools!" said the fourth. "Reality is a circle! Transcendental Consciousness is not Sleep, nor Dream, nor Wakefulness—but something beyond! It embraces the restful nothingness of Sleep, while being Awake: Self-Aware with no thought!"

"No, Reality is an ellipse!" said the fifth. "It has the Self-Awareness of the Circle, together with thought! In this way it can appreciate Itself as Cosmic Consciousness, the Silent Witness, embracing Sleep, and Dreaming, and Waking States!"

"No, Reality is a parabola!" said the sixth. "The Silent Witness of the Self has broken open into God-Consciousness, appreciating the infinite splendors of the Other—of the Supreme Lady-Lord of all of Creation!"

"No, no," said the seventh; "it's the hyperbola of Unity Consciousness! Two parabolas reflecting each other perfectly—the Self and the Lady-Lord know each other as One, and all of Creation is known as the Self!"

"An eighth Sage then appeared among them, holding a double-ended cone. "Here is Reality—a multidimensional *that* which each of you has been viewing through a single plane of consciousness—your ego! As soon as you realize *ALL* of these planes are transient, and *ALL* are simultaneously available, then you can surrender to the perfection of *THAT* which *IS* in this moment—*THAT* which is simultaneously a point, a line, an X, a circle, an ellipse, parabola, and a hyperbola! All seven of these states of Consciousness are but slices of *THAT!*"

—Rory Goff
Survival of Consciousness

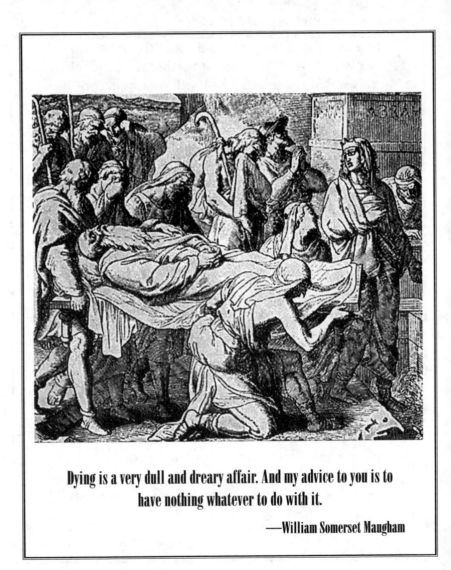

Dying is a very dull and dreary affair. And my advice to you is to have nothing whatever to do with it.

—William Somerset Maugham

2

WHAT IS DEATH?

Death is a process rather than an event because there is no single moment when a person dies. Death occurs when the heart stops beating and body is deprived of oxygen, which triggers a cascade of cellular death, beginning with brain cells and ending with skin cells.

> The boundaries between life and death are at best shadowy and vague. Who shall say where one ends and where the other begins?
>
> —Edgar Allen Poe

THE DEATH BED

We watched her breathing through the night,
Her breathing soft and low,
As in her breast the wave of life
Kept heaving to and fro.

So silently we seemed to speak,
So slowly moved about,
As we had lent her half our powers
To eke her living out.

Our very hopes belied our fears,
Our fears our hopes belied—
We thought her dying when she slept,
And sleeping when she died.

For when the morn came, dim and sad,
And chill with early showers,
Her quiet eyelids closed—
She had another morn than ours.

—Thomas Hood

Signs of Death

Traditionally, the signs of death were the absence of a heartbeat and breathing, and the onset of putre-faction. Extremities go numb, the body organs fail in domino fashion, the head falls from the back forward, and skin tone grays to a colorless paste. Body openings ooze. There is a loud death rattle like a deep throaty *"arrgh"* as the body jerks, then collapses. The shell cools as emptiness spreads a cloak of silence. Some report that death is accompanied by an odor, such as musk or after-shave perfume-like scent of roses, other times there may be a noxious smell.

Even with all of these indicators, it is not always easy to determine that a person is *really* dead. There are reports that some people have been buried when they were actually still "alive".

> Death is certain, since it is inevitable, but also uncertain, since its diagnosis sometimes fallible.
>
> —Jacques-Benigne Winslow
> *Morte Incertae Signa*

In 1742 John Bruhier documented fifty-two examples of live burials, in his book *Dissertation de L'incertitude des Signes de la Mort.*

By the end of the 19th Century, hysteria over fears of being buried alive grew to such a degree that over thirty different "safety coffins" had been patented in Germany. Each featured a mechanism to allow the mistakenly buried person to communicate with people above ground. Sometimes escape was achieved by pulling ropes which rang a loud bell. Other safety coffins were equipped with a fire cracker or other shooting device to draw attention to the person's plight. Sometimes a shovel, ladder and supply of food and water were included in the coffin. Later models featured a breathing tube to provide air until help could be summoned.

In 1822, amidst great fanfare, Dr. Adolf Gutsmuth had himself buried alive in his safety coffin to demonstrate its features. While buried underground for several hours he had a meal of soup, beer, and sausages served through a special feeding tube.

Have me decently buried, but do not let my body be put into a vault in less than two days after I am dead.
—George Washington
Dying Request

Such fears of premature burial placed pressure on doctors to identify more reliable signs of death. German doctors concluded that putrefaction was the only reliable indicator of death. To make sure that a person is truly dead before burial, a number of cultures require that there be an interval between death and disposal of the body to allow time for putrefaction. For example, in 19th century Germany bodies were taken to a leichenhäuser (corpse house) to be held until putrefaction was apparent.

There is no precise moment of death. Instead forensic scientists use clues for estimating the time of death. The first clue, of course, is lack of a pulse.

Signs of Death

1. Heart stops beating and/or lungs stop breathing.

2. Body cells no longer receive supplies of blood and oxygen. Brain cells can die if deprived of oxygen for more than three minutes. Blood drains from capillaries in the upper surfaces and collects in the blood vessels in the lower surfaces. Upper surfaces of the body become pale and the lower surfaces become dark.

3. Cells eventually die and the body loses its capacity to fight off bacteria. Muscle cells live on for several hours. Bone and skin cells can stay alive for several days.

4. Cells cease aerobic respiration and are unable to generate the energy molecules needed to maintain normal muscle biochemistry. Calcium ions leak into muscle cells preventing muscle relaxation. Rigor mortis, which is a stiffening of the muscles, sets in after three hours and lasts until 36 hours after death.

After a body has died, the chemical reaction producing these energy molecules is unable to proceed because of a lack of oxygen. The cells no longer have the energy to pump calcium out of the cell and so the calcium concentration rises, forcing the muscles to remain in a contracted state. This state of muscle stiffening is known as rigor mortis and it remains until the muscle proteins start to decompose.

5. The cells' own enzymes and bacterial activity cause the body to decompose and the muscles lose their stiffness.

6. It takes around 12 hours for a human body to be cool to the touch and 24 hours to cool to the core.

Religious Death

It remains for the doctor and especially the anesthesiologist, to give a clear and precise definition of "death" and the "moment of death" of a patient who passes away in a state of unconsciousness.

—Pope Pius XII

In 1957 Pope Pius XII raised the concerns over whether doctors might be "continuing the resuscitation process, despite the fact that the soul may already have left the body." He even asked one of the central questions confronting modern medicine, namely whether "death had already occurred after grave trauma to the brain, which has provoked deep unconsciousness and central breathing paralysis, the fatal consequences of which have been retarded by artificial respiration." The answer, he said, "did not fall within the competence of the Church."

Followers of religions like Zen Buddhism, and Shintoism believe that the mind and body are integrated and have trouble accepting the brain death criteria to determine death. Some Orthodox Jews, Native Americans, Muslims and fundamentalist Christians believe that as long as a heart is beating—even artificially, one is still alive.

For the Roman Catholic Church death is the "complete and final separation of the soul from the body". However the Vatican has conceded that diagnosing death is a subject for medicine, not the Church.

A medical diagnosis of "death" is not so straightforward, however. Medical advancements like the invention of the artificial respirator turned science's certainty about when death occurred upside down because cells can now be kept alive in the absence of breathing or of a natural heartbeat. Then with the first heart transplant in 1968, a reliable diagnosis for death not based on heartbeat was needed and medicine created the concept of "brain death".

Brain Death Diagnosis

◊ There is no evidence of brain function.

◊ The loss of function is not a result of drugs, low temperature—*hypothermia*, low blood sugar—*hypoglycaemia* or low blood sodium—*hyponatraemia*.

◊ A CT scan shows a brain injury is sufficient to account for the irreversible loss of brain function.

◊ Coughing, gagging, eye movement, blinking, or dilation of the pupils do not trigger any reflex.

◊ No attempt to breathe when disconnected from the respirator, and carbon dioxide level of the blood is above the point at where breathing is stimulated.

Attitudes and Beliefs

Arnold Toynbee developed typologies of orientations toward life and death based upon his cross-cultural studies of the many facets of death. Death is surrounded in rituals steeped in taboos. For most of us being in the presence of death is unsettling, even frightening. Death is often hidden, sanitized and orderly. Where did the person go? we ask in a whisper.

"Death" is a socially constructed idea. The fears and attitudes we have towards it are learned from educational and cultural vehicles such as the languages, arts, and religion. Every culture has its own explanation of death. What lessons can we learn from the examination of death as a social and cultural fact?

Toynbee found that some cultures can be death-accepting, death-denying or even death-defying. Death may be considered as the end of existence, or as a transition to another state of being or consciousness. Death can be viewed as sacred or profane, a state or process perceived to be sacrosanct or polluting for the living.

In the West, strategies for salvation focus on activism and asceticism which compliments our death-defying attitude towards death. By contrast, in the East strategies are more contemplative and mystical. For Buddhists and Hindus, the arch-ordeal envisioned is the pain of another rebirth rather than death.

Cultural Indicators of Attitudes

- Nature of the beliefs toward the meaning of life, death and the hereafter;
- Funerary rituals and strategies for body disposal;
- Physical and symbolic boundaries between the worlds of the living and the dead;
- Perceived role of the dead on the affairs of the living;
- Degree of social stigma attached to those dying, dead, or bereaved;
- Attitudes toward and rates of suicide, murder and abortion;
- Death prevention and avoidance as a social goal;
- Death socialization of children, death themes in children's stories and games and their involvement in funerary ritual;
- Taboo status of the topic of dying and death in everyday discourse;
- Language used regarding death;
- Nature and conceptions of death in the arts and media.

WHAT IT FEELS LIKE TO DIE

Your body goes limp. Your heart stops. No more air flows in or out. You lose sight, feeling, and movement—although the ability to hear goes last. Identity ceases. The "you" that you once were becomes only a memory. There is no pain at the moment of death. Only peaceful silence...calm...quiet. But you still exist. It is easy not to breathe. In fact, it is easier, more comfortable, and infinitely more natural not to breathe than to breathe.

The biggest surprise for most people in dying is to realize that dying does not end life. Whether darkness or light comes next, or some kind of event, be it positive, negative, or somewhere in-between, expected or unexpected, the biggest surprise of all is to realize you are still you. You can still think, you can still remember, you can still see, hear, move, reason, wonder, feel, question, and tell jokes —if you wish. You are still alive, very much alive. Actually, you're more alive after death than at any time since you were last born.

Only the way of all this is different; different because you no longer wear a dense body to filter and amplify the various sensations you had once regarded as the only valid indicators of what constitutes life. You had always been taught one has to wear a body to live.

—P.M.H. Atwater
We Live Forever

Legal Death

In western law, a person can be pronounced dead in three ways. Most common is pronouncement by a medical doctor. Second is pronouncement by a coroner or a medical examiner. Third, a person can be pronounced legally dead by the courts. After having disappeared for some time, the courts can pronounce one to be "legally dead" so that their property can be distributed appropriately. A death certificate is a legal document that describes how and when a person died, and who pronounced the death.

Life and subsequent death with its release of consciousness is merely part of an ongoing process: the development of consciousness, or spirit, within and without the body.

—Timothy Owe
Beyond Death

Death is feared as birth is forgotten.

—Doug Horton

3

Fear of Death

Death often arrives as a result of a traumatic event. Other times it comes after suffering from infirmities of age, disease or injury. When unexpected, such as when dying in an accident or from violence, death is shocking and traumatic. Family and friends suffer the pain of loss. The Scriptures in the Corinthians call death "the last enemy" to be conquered.

> Death is the last enemy: once we've got past that I think everything will be alright.
>
> —Alice Thomas Ellis

The Grim Reaper

In Western cultures, death is often given the name the "Grim Reaper", and shown as a skeletal figure carrying a large scythe, and wearing a midnight black gown, robe or cloak with a hood, or sometimes, a white burial shroud. Usually when portrayed in the black-hooded gown, only his eyes can be seen or nothing at all for that matter.

> You can be a king or a street sweeper, but everybody dances with the Grim Reaper.
>
> —Robert Alton Harris

Though descriptions vary somewhat, the basic entity is the same—a tall figure felt to be male wearing a long monks robe tied by rope at the waist, sometimes with a sickle or scythe, and sometimes without. A skeleton-like face is occasionally reported, but more often there is no discernible face and no visible extremities.

The face area is often described as being the darkest dark—almost a black abyss—sometimes with sparkling or shining areas where the eyes should be. When it moves, it seemingly glides rather than striding or walking.

What do we fear?

It has oft been said that "ignorance is bliss", but in the case of death, ignorance probably triggers the fear we experience when contemplating our last moments.

> We are ignorant of the Beyond because this ignorance is the condition of our own life. Just as ice cannot know fire except by melting and vanishing.
> —Pierre-Jules Renard

Knowing with certainty that we will die, yet not knowing what will actually happen is particularly vexing. It seems like hushed whispers and lack of information about death are part of a grand, but unspoken, conspiracy to deny death.

> American society expends a great deal of energy and resources to psychologically deny the reality of death. We treat it as unnatural, something that is not honestly talked about with the young in families and schools. We pay theological and medical professionals to handle it. When we do talk about it we cloak it in an aura of either a mystical "going home" or a "clinical cessation of biological life." It is neither of those.
> —Paul von Ward
> *Conscious Living and Dying*

Perhaps we would fare better if, like animals, we were ignorant of our certain death.

All our knowledge merely helps us to die a more painful death than animals that know nothing.

—*Maurice Maeterlinck*

Often the worry is not for ourselves, but for those who we leave behind—especially when they are children or beloved pets. We worry that they will suffer or will not be cared for. So we pay for life insurance month after month and "put our affairs in order".

A man's dying is more the survivors' affair than his own.

—Thomas Mann

Death is a tragedy... but only for the living. We who have died go on to other things.

—Charles de Lint
Into the Green

Some say that we cannot die. If that is true, why are we all so worried?

Though it be in the power of the weakest arm to take away life, it is not in the strongest to deprive us of death.

—Sir Thomas Browne

Death be not proud, though some have called thee mighty and dreadful, for thou art not so. For, those, whom thou think'st thou dost overthrow, die not, poore death, nor yet canst thou kill me.

—John Donne

Nothing, nothing, nothing at all

As we were nothing before we were conceived and eventually born, so too, upon death we return to that nothingness. Perhaps we had thoughts when in our mother's womb—certainly there were sensations. But before the successful sperm penetrated the egg to create our conception, we did not exist. We were nothing and had no consciousness. In death we merely return to that state of nothing.

Solomon said: For the living know that they will die; but the dead know nothing . . . .

—Ecclesiastes 9:5

DO WE SIMPLY CEASE TO BE?

Nothingness is a state of unawareness, of no consciousness. If it is nothing and there is no consciousness, then we can't possibly know when we have died or that we are dead.

To himself everyone is immortal; he may know that he is going to die, but he can never know that he is dead.

—Samuel Butler

If consciousness ceases at death and death is nothingness, then we have nothing to fear because we simply cease. We cannot suffer or worry. We simply are not. We return to dust—to nothingness

Death, feared as the most awful of evils, is really nothing. For so long as we are, death has not come, and when it has come we are not.

—Epicurus

Will I be bored?

There a notion that if there is a heaven and if heaven is good, then it must be boring. For some creative minds, being bored for eternity is thought to be worse than being nothing at all.

I don't believe in an afterlife, so I don't have to spend my whole life fearing hell, or fearing heaven even more. For whatever the tortures of hell, I think the boredom of heaven would be even worse.

—Isaac Asimov

Dear World, I am leaving because I am bored. I feel I have lived long enough. I am leaving you with your worries in this sweet cesspool. Good luck.

—George Sanders

Suicide note

Skeptics believe that religion teases us with the false hope of an afterlife. It is this false hope that causes our fears.

It took hundreds of years and thousands of lives, but the Universe finally taught me it's one and only lesson. Existence is worthless.

—Howard Weinstein

Religion teaches the dangerous non-sense that death is not the end.

—Richard Dawkins

Religion's Misguided Missiles

In the death is nothing view, when you're dead you cease and you are gone. Zip. Nothing. This is the pre-dominant view advanced in the West in our so-called modern times.

When you're dead, you're dead. That's it.
—Marlene Dietrich

I have wrestled with death. It is the most unexciting contest you can imagine. It takes place in an impalpable grayness, with nothing underfoot, with nothing around, without spectators, without clamor, without glory, without the great desire of victory, without the great fear of defeat.

—Joseph Conrad

Death is the end of sensuality, of feeling and enjoying. When the body dies, all fun and pleasure ends. We are thrown into nothingness.

A friend of mine stopped smoking, drinking, overeating, and chasing women—all at the same time. It was a lovely funeral.

—Unknown

For many just the thought of being in some state of eternal nothingness is frightening.

I wouldn't mind dying—it's the business of having to stay dead that scares the shit out of me.

—R. Geis

Death is an endless night so awful to contemplate that it can make us love life and value it with such passion that it may be the ultimate cause of all joy and all art.

—Paul Theroux

For others, there may be consolation in the idea that even though consciously we enter nothingness at death, our physical body continues on in some fashion. Our bodies can rot and become a kind of fertilizer nourishing plants and in this way we are not totally nothing. Perhaps our cells are transmuted into the pedals of a rose.

To cheat vegetation by locking up the gases upon which it feeds. By embalming their dead and thereby deranging the natural balance between animal and vegetable life, the Egyptians made their once fertile and populous country barren and incapable of supporting more than a meager crew. The modern metallic burial casket is a step in the same direction, and many a dead man who ought now to be ornamenting his neighbor's lawn as a tree, or enriching his table as a bunch of radishes, is doomed to a long inutility. We shall get him after awhile if we are spared, but in the meantime the violet and the rose are languishing for a nibble at his gluteus maximus.

—Ambrose Bierce

Boy, when you are dead, they really fix you up. I hope to hell when I do die somebody has sense enough to just dump me in the river or something. Anything except sticking me in a goddam cemetery. People coming and putting a bunch of flowers on your stomach on Sunday and all that crap. Who wants flowers when you are dead? Nobody.

—J.D. Salinger

After your death you will be what you were before your birth.

—Arthur Schopenhauer

When I die I shall be content to vanish into nothingness.... No show, however good, could conceivably be good forever.... I do not believe in immortality, and have no desire for it.

—H.L. Mencken

WiLL it HURt? WiLL I SUFFeR?

For others, it is not being dead and gone that is frightening. Nothingness can be accepted. What is feared is the transition—will it hurt? Will I suffer? I'm scared!

> I do not believe that any man fears to be dead, but only the stroke of death.
>
> —Francis Bacon

> It is not death, but dying, which is terrible.
>
> —Henry Fielding

> Life is pleasant. Death is peaceful.
> It's the transition that's troublesome.
>
> —Isaac Asimov

> I'm not afraid to die, I just don't want to be there when it happens.
>
> —Woody Allen

> Our soul, that animating spark of fire that is our core essence, does not fear death. Only our personality does.
>
> —P.M.H. Atwater
> *We Live Forever*

ENEMY OR SHAPE-SHIFTER?

If your belief system restricts your sense of identity to the confines of your physical body, I have noticed that death then becomes the enemy, robber of love and companionship, destroyer of time's cradle of opportunity. But if you recognize that all of us are more than our bodies (and we are), death becomes instead the shape shifter, guardian of spirit's journey through physical matter, restorer of vision and truth.

——P.M.H. Atwater
We Live Forever

Perhaps what is so unsettling and frightening about dying is our loss of control. When alive, we are in charge of our lives. But as we approach death, we may have become weakened by age and illness. At the moment of death, we are helpless. We can do nothing at all—except to pass away.

Dying is the most embarrassing thing that can ever happen to you, because someone's got to take care of all your details.

—Andy Warhol

Dying is almost un-American. We Americans don't like limits, we don't like boundaries. And death is the ultimate limit and the final boundary. We just would prefer not to talk about it.

—Bill Moyers

When a caterpillar dies, a butterfly is born.
—Bill & Judy Guggenheim
Hello From Heaven!

4

Death is a Transition

We living tend to think of death as an all or nothing event, finite and final. But death is actually a process in the continuum of existence between birth and death. Death cannot be separated from life, nor can life be separated from death.

The continuum of existence between birth and death is something like the space between sleeping and waking. Moving from one to the other is really a gradual process. Each step takes us to the next. Living and dying, breathing, sleeping, dreaming, being, communicating—our consciousness touches all of these worlds.

—Jeffrey Mishlove
Roots of Consciousness

Death is a pause, not an end—a transition from one mode of existence to another. But because we cannot see what is beyond the pause it feels like the end.

Death is not a period, but a comma in the story of life.

—Amos Traver

Death is a transition in an ongoing, never ending process. What is constant is consciousness, as it develops and evolves.

Death is but a transition from this life to another existence where there is no more pain and anguish. All the bitterness and disagreements will vanish, and the only thing that lives forever is *love*. So love each other *now*, for we never know how long we will be blessed with the presence of those who gave us life—no matter how imperfect many a parent has been.

—Elisabeth Kubler-Ross
On Life After Death

Contemplating death is difficult; talking about it even harder. We don't have the metal hooks. Metaphors help. One metaphor is to liken death to stepping into the next room. Deceased loved ones continue to exist—just on the other side of a divide where they await for the rest of us to follow.

Death is no more than passing from one room into another. But there's a difference for me, you know. Because in that other room I shall be able to see.

–Helen Keller

Death is a doorway from one room into another—a portal that we pass through that changes us, yet we still exist—only in a different form—in an adjoining room, waiting. Perhaps passing through the gates of death is like passing quietly through the gate in a pasture fence. On the other side, you keep walking, without the need to look back. No shock, no drama, just the lifting of a plank or two in a simple wooden gate in a clearing. Neither pain, nor floods of light, nor great voices, but just the silent crossing of a meadow.

–Mark Helprin
A Soldier of the Great War

Death Is Nothing At All

Death is nothing at all

I have only slipped away into the next room

I am I and you are you

Whatever we were to each other

That we are still

Call me by my old familiar name

Speak to me in the easy way you always used

Put no difference into your tone

Wear no forced air of solemnity or sorrow

Laugh as we always laughed

At the little jokes we always enjoyed together

Play, smile, think of me, pray for me

Let my name be ever the household word that it
always was

Let it be spoken without effort

Without the ghost of a shadow in it

Life means all that it ever meant

It is the same as it ever was

There is absolute unbroken continuity

What is death but a negligible accident?

Why should I be out of mind

Because I am out of sight?

I am waiting for you for an interval

Somewhere very near

Just around the corner

All is well.

Nothing is past; nothing is lost

One brief moment and all will be as it was before

How we shall laugh at the trouble of parting when
we meet again!

—Canon Henry Scott-Holland
St Paul's Cathedral

Leaving our body at the moment of death can be thought of as being like a tenant moving out of an old house into a new one in a neighboring town.

I can remember how when I was young I believed death to be a phenomenon of the body; now I know it to be merely a function of the mind—and that of the minds of the ones who suffer the bereavement. The nihilists say it is the end; the fundamentalists, the beginning; when in reality it is no more than a single tenant or family moving out of a tenement or a town.

—William Faulkner
As I Lay Dying

THERE IS NO DEATH! WHAT SEEMS SO IS TRANSITION; THIS LIFE OF MORTAL BREATH IS BUT A SUBURB OF THE LIFE ELYSIAN, WHOSE PORTAL WE CALL DEATH.

—HENRY W. LONGFELLOW

Death is just a change in lifestyles.

—Stephen Levine

Another appealing metaphor is to liken the body to an automobile and the spirit or soul to the driver. Both are vehicles that carry us on a journey. When the car wears out we can leave it on the side of the road. Similarly when the bodily vehicle wears out, the soul steps out and leaves the no longer needed physical body on the side of the road.

Dying is like getting out of a car. You leave a shell behind, but you're the same person as ever.   —President Klein

A physical body may be compared to an automobile, for both are "vehicles" we use for traveling through life. A few are defective when they are new and break down quickly, while some receive poor care from their owners and deteriorate rapidly or are destroyed in an accident. However, most vehicles require only regular maintenance and minor repairs. Naturally, all cars and physical bodies eventually wear out and have to be disposed of. But when this occurs, we needn't perceive that the driver of a car or the wearer of a body ceases to exist as well.

—Bill & Judy Guggenheim
Hello From Heaven

METAMORPHOSIS

Thinking of death as a metamorphosis is comforting. We live and develop in a protective cocoon, never imagining that one day we will emerge as a beautiful wondrous butterfly.

There are two bodies—the rudimental and the complete; corresponding with the two conditions of the worm and the butterfly. What we call "death", is but the painful metamorphosis.

—Edgar Allan Poe
Mesmeric Revelation

Death of the human body is identical to what happens when the butterfly emerges from its cocoon. The cocoon can be compared to the human body, but is not identical with your real self for it is only a house to live in for a while. Dying is only moving from one house into a more beautiful one.

—Elisabeth Kubler-Ross
On Life After Death

D eath being akin to an infant bird gestating in the egg from which it will one day emerge is another comforting metaphor.

Just as a little bird cracks open the shell and flies out, we fly out of this shell, the shell of the body. We call that death, but strictly speaking, death is nothing but a change of form.

—Swami Satchidananda

We wear an earth suit that we discard at death like tossing a worn tee-shirt into the hamper.

You live on earth only for a few short years which you call an incarnation, and then you leave your body as an outworn dress and go for refreshment to your true home in the spirit.

—White Eagle

Death is returning home after a long trip in a strange land.

Death is not the end, it is simply walking out of the physical form and into the spirit realm, which is our true home. It's going back home.

-Stephen Christopher

Death is a transition as we shed the distresses of living.

Death is a transition.... Helen Keller will see and hear. The child who died of cancer will have rosy cheeks and a strong body. The man crippled with arthritis will stand upright. The woman who was disfigured in a fiery car crash will have a face without blemish.

—Dr. Billy Graham

Skeptics insist that nobody who hasn't died can talk about death with authority. Since nobody has ever returned from death, we cannot know what death is, or what happens after we die.

In the Tibetan view we have all returned from death, having died many deaths, before we coming into this incarnation. Birth is the reverse side of death, like one side of a coin, or like a door we pass through.

It is ... astonishing that not everybody remembers his or her previous death; and, because of this lack of remembering, most persons do not believe there was a previous death. But, likewise, they do not remember their recent birth—and yet they do not doubt that they were recently born. They forget that active memory is only a small part of our normal consciousness, and that our subconscious memory registers and preserves every past impression and experience which our waking mind fails to recall.

—Lama Anagarika Govinda
The Tibetan Book of the Dead

THERE IS NO DEATH

There is an ebb and flow, a rhythm, a cycle to everything in the Universe. So too with life and death.

There is no death. The stars go down to rise upon some other shore. And bright in Heaven's jeweled crown, they shine for ever more.

—John Luckey McCreery

Die happily and look forward to taking up a new and better form. Like the sun, only when you set in the west can you rise in the east.

—Jelaluddin Rumi

The call of death is a call of love. Death can be sweet if we answer it in the affirmative, if we accept it as one of the great eternal forms of life and transformation.

—Hermann Hesse

Celebrate the Transition!

The moment when someone leaves his or her body is often sad for all of us who are left behind. Luckily, the experience is very different for the spirit actually making the transition. From what I have seen and learned in my years of speaking with those who have had near-death experiences, I believe the time of transition is a celebration—sort of like an Irish wake, with our departed loved ones waiting for us with open arms on the other side.

—Char Margolis
Questions From Earth
Answers From Heaven

I am standing upon the seashore. A ship at my side spreads her white sails to the ocean. She is an object of beauty and strength. I stand and watch her until at length she hangs like a speck of white cloud just where the sea and sky come to mingle with each other. Then someone at my side says: "There, she is gone!" "Gone where?" Gone from my sight. That is all. Her diminished size is in me, not in her. And just at the moment when someone at my side says: "There, she is gone!" there are other eyes watching her coming, and other voices ready to take up the glad shout: "Here she comes!" And that is dying.
—Henry Van Dyke

Death, the last sleep? No, the final awakening.

—Sir Walter Scott

5

AWAKENING

S ages and philosophers tell us that while living we are actually in a kind of sleep that creates an illusion to hide who we really are. But at death we awaken!

We sometimes congratulate ourselves at the moment of waking from a troubled dream; it may be so at the moment after death.

—Nathaniel Hawthorne

Life is a great sunrise. I do not see why death should not be an even greater one.

—Vladimir Nobokov

When we awaken we become aware of what is *really* going on. We "remember" what we had forgotten and had hidden from ourselves—*who we really are!*

All your life you think you are your body.
Some of the time you think you are you mind.
It is at the time of your death that you find out
Who You Really Are.

—Neale Donald Walsch
Conversations with God

The soul arrives in the light, where you see with complete clarity for the first time to realize the truth of existence that was masked by being in a physical body.

Know that life is a continuous experience, and as there is a consciousness in sleep that is not physical—in the sense of physical awareness—so there is a consciousness in the same manner when the physical is entirely laid aside....

—*Edgar Cayce*

The major trick in this deception is, of course, death. Consider death as the permanent end of consciousness, the point at which you and your knowledge of the universe simple cease, and where you become as if you had never existed at all. Consider it also on a much vaster scale—the death of the universe at the time when all energy runs out, ... It will be as if it never happened, which is, of course, the way things were before it *did* happen. Likewise, when you are dead, you will be as you were before you were conceived.

But if, when it has happened and vanished, things are as they were before it began, it can happen again. Why not? ... I find it difficult to think of a single, particular time when it had to stop. Can anything be half eternal? That is, can a process which had no beginning come to an end?

For eternity and always there is only *now*, one and the same now; the present is the only thing that has no end.

—Alan W. Watts
The Book
On the Taboo Against Knowing Who You Are

✂—◎—✂

Awakening

As we awaken we discover that there is no there there; it has been here all along—here and now. Heaven is here and now—eternally.

There is no such thing as "getting to heaven". There is only a knowing that you are already there. There is an accepting, an understanding, not a working for or a striving.

You cannot go to where you already are. To do that, you would have to leave where you are, and that would defeat the whole purpose of the journey.

The irony is that most people think that they have to leave where they are to get to where they want to be. And so they leave heaven in order to get to heaven—and go through hell.

Enlightenment is understanding that there is nowhere to go, nothing to do, and nobody you have to be except exactly who you're being right now.

You are on a journey to nowhere.

Heaven—as you call it—is nowhere. Let's just put some space between the *w* and the *h* in that word and you'll see that heaven is now...here.

—Neale Donald Walsch
Conversations with God

What is this all about?

What did we forget? Why do we live in an illusion? What are we hiding from? What does the soul want anyway?

This is It
And I am It
And You are It
And so is That
And He is It
And She is It
And It is It
And That is That.

—Alan W Watts
The Book
On the Taboo Against Knowing Who You Are

Why do we have a soul, anyway? For what purpose? What is going on? Why must we live with illusions and forgetting?

The purpose of the human soul is to experience all of it——so that it can be all of it.

—Neale Donald Walsch
Conversations with God

Are we seeking to be God?

Of course you are seeking to be God!

What else did you think you were up to?

—Neale Donald Walsch
Conversations with God

We are not human beings having a spiritual experience, we are spiritual beings having a human experience.

—Dr. Wayne W. Dyer

WHat can I expect?

Probably the most worrisome thing about dying is not knowing what to expect. PMH Atwater, who "died" three times and came back, says that we don't die, we merely slough off the body.

If you expect to die when you die you will be disappointed. The only thing dying does is help you release, slough off, and discard the "jacket" you once wore (more commonly referred to as a body). When you die you lose your body. That's all there is to it. Nothing else is lost.

—P.M.H. Atwater
We Don't Die

Of course you don't die. Nobody dies. Death doesn't exist. You only reach a new level of vision, a new realm of consciousness, a new unknown world.

—Henry Miller

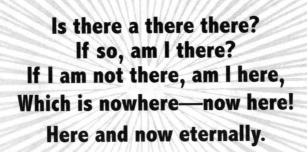

Is there a there there?
If so, am I there?
If I am not there, am I here,
Which is nowhere—now here!
Here and now eternally.

What Does a Butterfly Expect?

In its wildest dreams a caterpillar is not aware of its potential to fly. By shedding its skin, it can grow wings, become a butterfly, and partake of a whole new dimension of life. Our caterpillar may be apprehensive about the necessity to change. It seems like death, but dying as a caterpillar it resurrects as a butterfly! We cannot realize or imagine the consciousness and might of the Absolute—whether we call it God or another name—the real reason and creative force acting in all dimensions, although mankind has received descriptions of divine cosmic laws from enlightened teachers throughout the ages.

—Roza Riaikkenen
—Andrew Rooke
Beyond Caterpillar Consciousness

I think I will enter a realm of pure consciousness, and I am hoping that my death will be as conscious as my life. And at that moment, I will be able to make the choices that I want about where I want to evolve and how I want to evolve as I make them now.

—Deepak Chopra

Denying the afterlife isn't rooted in scientific fact, it is rooted in belief.

6

WHAT ABOUT SCIENCE?

In 1687 Isaac Newton described gravity and the three laws of motion, laying the groundwork for classical mechanics, which has dominated the scientific view of the physical universe for the last three centuries. Newton showed that the motions of objects on Earth and of celestial bodies are governed by the same set of natural laws.

Newtonian physics is the bedrock of what we believe is real and how things work. In this materialistic view, consciousness evolved from a random, blind-chance process. There is no afterlife after we die. When the body dies, consciousness dies with it. Death is final because life exists only in the physical body.

Even though we have sophisticated microscopes and telescopes that extend the power of our senses, the majority of scientists still hold the classical Newtonian view of the universe.

Modern science, in general, either describes the universe and human beings without reference to a soul or to an afterlife, or tends to remain mute on the issue.
—Gary Zukav

The Dancing Wu Li Masters
An Overview of the New Physics

In the classical scientific view existence is explained solely in material terms. There is no spirit or consciousness separate from the physical body.

The problem is that neuroscientists do not know what consciousness is and have no theories to explain its nature. That is because our science is the science of the external world, a hangover from the time of the Renaissance, and it does not deal with subjective experience, or with consciousness. This is the main problem facing neuroscience at the moment, and it may well be that NDE research will be one way of filling the "consciousness gap" in neuroscience.
—Peter Fenwick, M.D.

In the Newtonia view, the universe is a huge machine operating according to naturalistic laws. The Theory of Evolution explains creation of the universe, reality and how things work.

If all that exists is matter *only*, where did the natural laws that govern matter come from?

Denying the afterlife isn't scientific, it is actually a belief that everything is material—materialism.

Acceptance without proof is a fundamental characteristic of western religion. Rejection without proof is the fundamental characteristic of western science.

—**Gary Zukav**
The Dancing Wu Li Masters
An Overview of the New Physics

While spiritual and material views seem quite divergent, they still ring true because each speaks to part of our knowingness.

We have myths and stories. We have world views, paradigms, constructs and hypotheses. We have competing dogmas, theologies and sciences. Do we have understanding? Can an integration of our scientific knowledge with the spiritual insights of humanity bring greater harmony to human civilization?

—Jeffrey Mishlove
Roots of Consciousness

The Quantum World

Recent scientific discoveries in biological complexity, cosmological design, quantum physics, and information theory bring these materialistic assumptions into doubt. A massive quantity of evidence demonstrates that the universe and its material aspects are connected by a network of energy, design, and information.

> Common sense contradictions are at the heart of the new physics. They tell us again and again that the world may not be what we think it is. *It may be much, much more.*
>
> —Gary Zukav
> *The Dancing Wu Li Masters*
> *An Overview of the New Physics*

Quantum physics, which studies infinitesimally small subatomic particles, has demonstrated that movements and properties of subatomic objects do not follow the old ways of thinking found in classical physics developed by Sir Issac Newton and others.

Quantum physics turns our notions upside down.

At the sub-atomic level of existence,

Newtonian physics simply doesn't work!

Quantum space is a world of paradox and utter confusion where a thing both occupies a single place at a single time and occupies an infinite number of places at the same time.

At the sub-atomic level, particles don't simply move from point A to point B in a continuous fashion as they do in our Newtonian reality.

Subatomic particles move in "quantum jumps" leaping from one place to another.

Duh?

It's all an Illusion

Our human bodies seem solid, but are over 99.99% empty space. The universe being just matter and energy is an illusion created by our human senses— seeing, hearing, feeling, tasting, smelling.

Classical Newtonian physics says that there is one world, it is as it appears, and this is it. Quantum physics says this is possibility not so.

New Soul Physics

The old physics assumes that there is an external world that exists apart from us. But in the quantum world what is observed is determined by *who* is observing.

Consciousness is not separate from the matter of the universe—consciousness is creating it!!!

It is an illusion of perception that we are present inside our physical bodies looking out at the world.

There is no place inside your body where "you" actually exist. It is an illusion that everything outside that volume of space is "not you". A better description for this sense of presence is that *you are everywhere.*

You have some sense of being present in your body looking out at the world. But according to what we know from physics, this is an illusion of perception: There is no place inside your body where "you" actually exist. You don't have a particular volume of space or spot that is "you." It is an illusion to think that everything outside that volume of space is "not you"--what you commonly say is "outside of you." The best description we can give for this sense of presence is that you "are everywhere." The main reason that you have more awareness of being in a body is simply because the sensory apparatus of the body commands a great deal of your attention and that much of your attention is linked to your physical senses.

—Fred Alan Wolf
Dr. Quantum

Newton's Laws are based upon observations of the everyday world. They *predict events.* These events pertain to real things that can be reliably measured, like kitchen sinks and automobiles.

Quantum Mechanics is based upon experiments conducted in the subatomic realm, which can not be observed directly. They *predict probabilities.* Nothing is certain, only probable to a certain degree—depending upon who is watching and how they are measuring.

Man has the possibility of existence after death. But possibility is one thing and the realization of the possibility is quite a different thing.

— George Gurdjieff

Skepticism is not science

We assume that science disproves metaphysics and all invisible things associated with God—the soul, heaven, hell, and so on. This assumption is skepticism, not science. With the introduction of quantum physics science has come to accept the existence of invisible worlds.

Before we knew quantum physics we thought that consciousness simply was an accompaniment to the objective world, that it played no role other than taking notes, mapping the external world, and storing data as memory. The "out there" was indeed out there and had no connection with mind.

But with quantum physics we found that *consciousness actually acts on the physical world. It makes its mark so that the world is not and cannot be the same without consciousness present.* Hence consciousness performs a dual role in the universe.

In the world of quantum physics, *it forms at once both the awareness and the creation of experience.* Each act of consciousness not only marks for memory the event of awareness noted but through the *principle of complementarity*—namely that *the observer changes the observed by the way the observation is performed—it creates the event noted.*

—Fred Alan Wolf
Dr. Quantum

Everything science has taught me strengthens my belief in the continuity of our spiritual existence after death. I believe in an immortal soul. Science has proved that nothing disintegrates into nothingness. Life and soul, therefore, cannot disintegrate into nothingness, and so are immortal.

—WERNER VON BRAUN

Quantum physics is stranger than science fiction, revealing at least eleven dimensions and parallel universes with different editions of us living in many worlds simultaneously—an uncountable number of them—and all of them are real.

Quantum theory boldly states that something can be this and that— both a wave and a particle.

The evidence gathered in the development of quantum mechanics indicates that subatomic "particles" constantly appear to be making decisions! More than that, the decision they seem to make are based on decisions made elsewhere. Subatomic particles seem to know *instantaneously.* How can a subatomic particle over here know what decision another particle over there has made *at the same time the particle over there makes it?* All evidence belies the fact that quantum particles are actually particles.

—Gary Zukav
Dancing Wu Li Masters

WE DO NOT SEE LIFE AS IT REALLY IS

The world is an illusion, not in the sense that it does not exist, but illusory in the sense that we do not see it as it *really* is. The rational mind superimposes its rules on data coming in from the senses to create its own version of what must be.

Some people have difficulty accepting that something can be real but not physical. Is there anything in science that is real but not physical? The effects of magnetism clearly demonstrates that something may exist, is real, is not physical and solid, yet it can fill space and move in time——as we know magnetic fields do. If a common phenomenon like a magnetic field acting on iron filings can do this, could not the soul be an invisible, non-material, super-intelligent, animating force that similarly acts on and through the human body and the universe?

——Fred Alan Wolf
Dr. Quantum

What we perceive to be physical reality is actually our cognitive construction of it.

The findings of quantum physics increasingly . . . suggests the existence of a non-material, non-physical universe that has a reality even though it is not clearly perceptible to our senses and scientific instrumentation. When we consider out-of-body experiences, shamanic journeys, and lucid dream states, though they cannot be replicated in the true scientific sense, they also point to the existence of non-material dimensions of reality.

—Fred Alan Wolf
Dr. Quantum

. . . .If you expect to die when you die, you will be disappointed.

—P.M.H. Atwater

7

NEAR-DEATH EXPERIENCE

According to a Gallup Poll, more than thirteen million Americans have had a near-death experience (NDE) where they clinically died and then were revived.

During this limbo period "experiencers"—people experiencing a NDE—believe that they actually died and came back. People report having encounters with spirit guides, seeing dead relatives or friends, feelings of total serenity, security, warmth, and a detachment from the body. A life review is common, along with the presence of an intense, pure light that seems like a deity or spiritual presence, and a moment of decision where they decide or are told to turn back to earthly life.

After having had three near-death experiences, P.M.H. Atwater has devoted her career to researching the intriguing phenomena in which she has interviewed over 3000 people who have had a "near-death experience".

Expectations about death are shaped by our earthly existence in a physical body.

....You have always been taught that
in order to live you have to wear a body.

You are not your body. It is just something you wear for a while, because living in the earth plane is infinitely more meaningful and more involved if you are encased in its trappings and subject to its rules.

—P.M.H. At Water
We Live Forever

NDEs suggest that some aspect of human consciousness may continue after physical death.

Near-death experiences point toward consciousness beyond death. The brain identity theory says that consciousness ends with brain death. But if it can be shown that people can acquire information when they are unconscious and out of their body and if deathbed coincidences are real, it would be indisputable evidence that consciousness is separate from the brain.

—Peter Fenwick, M.D.

The question is:

"Do near-death experiences show that consciousness can exist outside of the physical body?"

If this can be proven true, the next question is:

"Can consciousness survive bodily death?"

Experiencers tell of passing through a dark tunnel, then refocusing and becoming aware of a detached spiritual body watching the physical body with revival efforts underway. Subsequently a world filled with light and freedom emerges in which the individual meets a "being of light" who portrays perfect understanding and love, leaving them with a deep sense of peace and well-being.

Almost to a person experiencers return knowing that "God is, death isn't", a realization of profound significance.

—P.M.H. At water
we Live Forever

Experiencers often revive with a knowing or having been told that it isn't their time to die, that they have a job to do— a mission yet to perform here in this life.

"It's not your time yet," indicates that each of us may have a spiritual purpose for your life and a sufficient amount of time to achieve it. It implies there is a larger objective and a deeper meaning for everyone's existence than mere day-to-day physical survival.

—Bill & Judy Guggenheim
Hello From Heaven

Like Flipping the Dial

A twater reported that there seems to be a step-up of energy at the moment of death, an increase in speed as if you are suddenly vibrating faster than before.

Using radio as an analogy, Atwater describes this speed-up as comparable to having lived all your life at a certain radio frequency when all of a sudden someone flips the dial, which shifts you to another, higher wavelength. The original frequency where you once existed is still there. It did not change. Everything is still just the same as it was. Only you changed, only you speeded up to allow entry into the next radio frequency on the dial.

What I found once I left the world of time and space during my death episodes were countless realms and dimensions of existence that ranged from the slower, more dense vibrations to shape and sound (similar to being inside rocks or metal) to higher, finer streamers of nonenergetic currents and abstractions .... These realms and dimensions existed in field arrays of wave forms (orderly domains). They appeared as a layered matrix. The various levels of each plane were separated from each other by frequencies of vibration.

—P.M.H. At Water

We Live Forever

So at the time of death, or during a near-death experience, it may very well be that the person transitions from the material world—that operates at speeds less than the speed of light—to a world that operates faster than light speed, the so-called "superluminal" spiritual world. In that transfer, a tunneling effect may take place in much the same way that it appears to take place in what astrophysicists call a "black hole." Now this is where it gets really interesting. At the superluminal speed of the soul, we go beyond time and space as we experience it in this physical dimension. We then have the phenomenon of being able to move both forward and backward through time/space. People who come back from a near-death experience describe something like this. What these people are very likely experiencing are windows into that kind of time/space dimension of reality.

—Fred Alan Wolf
Dr. Quantum

I no longer fear death itself. In near-death (and, by extrapolation, in death itself), I think you find the answer to the question you've most been looking for. Although mine wasn't one of the blissful near-death experiences I have since read about, neither was it at all frightening; it was, rather, by far the calmest moment of my life, deeply centering.

—David J. Bookbinder
Beyond Blue

Not Really Dead!

When a person returns to life, the scientific or medical conclusion is that the patient obviously was not dead after all, but only near death. The reason that they were *near death* rather than *really dead* derives, at least in part, from the assumption that one cannot return from "real" death.

In his research, Dr. Ken Ring's found that experiencers often witness events and hear conversations from great distances which were later verified.

An even more fascinating phenomenon occurs when, during a NDE, the experiencer actually appears in spirit to someone, usually a loved one, and it is verified to be true by the experiencer and the loved one.

Evidence such as this, if scientifically replicated, that could provide proof that consciousness can exist outside of the body. While science does not yet have the tools to accomplish this, science is coming very, very close.

A Normal Process

Though an NDE may be caused by an injury or disease and it may have disorienting effects somewhat like a mental illness, near-death is neither a mental illness nor a disease. It is a process we go through, I believe, when our minds become aware that we are dying. Something monumental happens then, and it happens very fast.   —Peter Novak

The most common descriptions I have found of the moment when death occurs is that there is a feeling of coldness and then suddenly the spirit is standing by the side of the bed (or whatever) looking at their body. They usually can't understand why the other people in the room are so upset because they feel so wonderful. The overall sensation is one of exhilaration rather than dread.

—Dolores Cannon
Between Death & Life

According to physicist, David Bohm, the energy of the universe is not a neutral energy; it is an energy of love.

When we are born, we emerge out of the constriction of the womb and birth canal into the wondrous world of previously unimaginable and virtually unlimited sensory experience. And when we die, we go through a second birth, which may be even more difficult than the first, leave the world we know for another that transcends anything we can conceive where we discover, finally, what it is to be alive. Fully alive, and filled with a radiant joy "beyond the realm of happiness." This is the message those who have made the journey have to tell those who are about to undertake it. It is the greatest gift that they have to share and, for some, the reason they have returned to life.

—Ken Ring
Lessons from the Light

Two interpretations of the near-death experience:

1. It is merely a delusion of a dying brain

2. It is our soul or consciousness disassociating itself from the dying body

I can say without hesitation that you encounter far more than you could possibly imagine when you die. Your previous beliefs do not necessarily determine what that is. Life is not as limiting as you may have though; neither is death. As near as I can tell, there is no end of discoveries and the encounters you can have beyond death. Truly, death is but a shift in consciousness—like a doorway through which we pass. What we find, no matter what this is, constitutes hardly more than a "wink" in infinity.

—P.M.H. Atwater
We Live Forever

OVER THE RIVER

Over the river they beckon to me,
Loved ones who've crossed to the farther side,
The gleam of their snowy robes I see,
But their voices are lost in the dashing tide.
There's one with ringlets of sunny gold,
And eyes the reflection of heaven's own blue;
He crossed in the twilight gray and cold,
And the pale mist hid him from mortal view.
We saw not the angels who met him there,
The gates of the city we could not see:
Over the river, over the river,
My brother stands waiting to welcome me.

Over the river the boatman pale
Carried another, the household pet;
Her brown curls waved in the gentle gale,
Darling Minnie! I see her yet.
She crossed on her bosom her dimpled hands,

And fearlessly entered the phantom bark;
We felt it glide from the silver sands,
And all our sunshine grew strangely dark;
We know she is safe on the farther side,
Where all the ransomed and angels be:
Over the river, the mystic river,
My childhood's idol is waiting for me.

For none returns from those quiet shores,
Who cross with the boatman cold and pale;
We hear the dip of the golden oars,
And catch a gleam of the snowy sail; And lo!
They have passed from our yearning hearts,
They cross the stream and are gone for aye.
We may not sunder the veil apart
That hides from our vision the gates of day;
We only know that their barks no more
May sail with us o'er life's stormy sea;
Yet somewhere, I know, on the unseen shore,
They watch, and beckon, and wait for me.

And I sit and think, when the sunset's gold
Is flushing river and hill and shore,
I shall one day stand by the water cold,
And listen for the sound of the boatman's oar;
I shall watch for a gleam of the flapping sail,
I shall hear the boat as it gains the strand,
I shall pass from sight with the boatman pale,
To the better shore of the spirit land.
I shall know the loved who have gone before,
And joyfully sweet will the meeting be,
When over the river, the peaceful river,
The angel of death shall carry me.

—Nancy Woodbury Priest

*a*ncient Egyptians believed each individual has two souls, a *ba* and a *ka*, which separate at death unless steps are taken to prevent this division. Other ancient cultures believed in two souls, one like the conscious, the other like the unconscious, which separate at death.

Some cultures held that one soul would go on to reincarnate, while the other would become trapped in a dreamlike netherworld.

The two stages of near-death experiences, a detached, objective, and dispassionate black void followed by a subjective, relationship-oriented, and emotionally intense realm of light, reflect the distinctions between the conscious mind and the unconscious mind.

The darkness stage seems to be experienced exclusively through the conscious half of the psyche, while the light stage seems to be experienced exclusively through the unconscious, as if the two were operating independently during these episodes.

no one can confidently
        say that he will still
be living tomorrow.

—Euripides

BETWEEN THE PEOPLE OF ETERNITY
AND THE PEOPLE OF THE EARTH THERE
IS CONSTANT COMMUNICATION.

—Kahlil Gibran

8

AFTER-DEATH COMMUNICATION

During the first days and weeks after a loved one "passes away" it is quite common for friends and family to receive what seem to be communications from them. Bill and Judy Guggenheim, leading researchers into the phenomena define an "after-death communication" (ADC) as a direct and spontaneous contact from a deceased family member or friend, without the use of psychics, mediums, rituals, or devices of any kind.

After-death communications can be experienced by children and adults of any age. Experiencers come from all social backgrounds and economic levels.

Based on their findings from over 2000 inter-views with those who said they were contacted in some manner by their loved ones after his or her death, the Guggenheims estimate that at least 50 million Americans—or 20 percent of the population—have had one or more credible after-death communication experiences.

It's estimated that 60-120 million Americans—20-40% of the population of the United States—have had one or more ADC experiences. Therefore, ADCs provide convincing new evidence for life after death.

—Bill Guggenheim and Judy Guggenheim
Hello from Heaven

While ADCs are usually experienced alone, they are occasionally witnessed by others. Sometimes there is a warning to the experiencer of an unknown but imminent danger. Often the communication includes information the experiencer did not previously know, such as the location of missing valuables like money or an heirloom.

A woman had a vision of her father who said, "It's all right, honey. It's beautiful over here, so don't you worry." He laughed, adding "Now I don't have to pay for all that furniture your mom and sister bought." Within minutes she got a phone call saying her father had just died of a heart attack. And not long afterward, she received a letter from her mother saying she and the sister had bought a house full of furniture right before her father died!

—Bill & Judy Guggenheim
Hello From Heaven

Communication with the departed often comes during a dream.

Six weeks after his death my father appeared to me in a dream.... It was an unforgettable experience, and it forced me for the first time to think about life after death.

-Carl G. Jung

Your relative or friend can come to you more easily when you are relaxed, open, and receptive, such as while you are in a meditative alpha state or when sleeping.

At night when we're sleeping, our soul will come out of our body and communicate, and our deceased loved ones will come and communicate with our soul. And then it comes through our conscious mind, but we just think it's a dream.

—Echo Bodine
Echoes of the Soul

THE DEAD

The dead abide with us! Though stark and cold

Earth seems to grip them, they are with us still:

They have forged our chains of being for good or ill;

And their invisible hands these hands yet hold.

Our perishable bodies are the mould

In which their strong imperishable will;

Mortality's deep yearning to fulfill;

Hath grown incorporate through dim time untold.

Vibrations infinite of life in death,

As a star's travelling light survives its star!

So may we hold our lives, that when we are

The fate of those who then will draw this breath,

They shall not drag us to their judgment-bar,

And curse the heritage which we bequeath.

—Mathilde Blind

Comforting

Loved ones left behind find comfort in after-death communications, especially those containing information only they could have known.

When someone is alone and overwhelmed by grief, life seems over. But, when I'm able to help teach someone to make contact with a loved one, their grief and loneliness disappears and proper closure can take place.

—James Van Praagh
Talking to Heaven

I'm here to tell you death is not the end. Almost every time I read for someone I can sense the presence of spirits around them. These spirits are usually the souls of loved ones who are no longer alive on this plane but who still exist and love on another level.

—Char Margolis
Questions from Earth
Answers from Heaven

Messages are almost always of comfort and appreciation, telling those left behind to not worry, that they are fine and will see them again when they pass over.

according to our research, the purpose of these visits and signs by those who have died is to offer comfort, reassurance, and hope to their parents, spouse, siblings, children, grandchildren, other family members, and friends. They want you to know they're still alive and that you'll be reunited with them when it's your time to leave this physical life on earth — and they'll be there to greet you when you make your transition.

—Bill & Judy Guggenheim
Hello From Heaven

Types of After-Death Communication

Sensing a Presence: Having a distinct feeling that your loved one is nearby.

Hearing a Voice: Most audio ADC communications are telepathic—the voice is heard in your mind.

Feeling a Touch: Feeling a tap, a pat, a caress, a stroke, a kiss, or even a hug.

Smelling a Fragrance: Smelling an after-shave lotion or perfume; scent of flowers (especially roses), bath powders, tobacco products, favorite foods reminiscent of the departed person.

Visual Apparitions: Appearances range from "a transparent mist" to "absolutely solid" with many gradations in between. The soul visitor may appear at the foot of the bed, inside or outdoors, in a car or aboard a plane.

Visions: Seeing an image of a deceased loved one in a flat "picture" or 3-D hologram suspended in air.

Twilight Experiences: Communications often come when in the alpha state—when falling asleep, waking up, meditating, or praying

Messages in Dreams: Sleep-state ADCs are more vivid, intense, colorful, and real than dreams. with both one-way and two-way communications. You usually feel your loved one is with you in person—that you're having an actual visit together. These experiences are not jumbled, filled with symbols, or fragmented the way dreams are.

Out-Of-Body Experiences: Leaving your body while sleeping or meditating to visit your loved one. Vivid and intense, feeling "more real than physical life" with beautiful flowers and butterflies, colorful bushes and trees, radiant lighting.

Telephone Calls: Hearing a phone ringing, when sleep or awake and when you answer your loved one gives a short message.

ASK FOR A SIGN

People often ask a Higher Power, the universe, or their deceased loved one for a sign that he or she still exists.

After Paul McCartney's wife Linda died he said he was comforted by thoughts that her spirit lives on. "After Linda died, I think all of us in the family would hear noises or see things and think 'That's Linda; that's mom...' And I think in some ways, it's very comforting to think she's still here."

—Paul McCartney
Good Morning America/ABC

The bereaved often report receiving a variety of physical signs from their deceased relative or friend, such as: lights or lamps blinking on and off; radios, televisions, stereos, and mechanical objects being turned on; photographs, pictures, and various other items being turned over or moved.

Other common signs include: butterflies, rainbows, many species of birds and animals, flowers, and a variety of inanimate objects such as coins and pictures.

McCartney wrote a poem called "Her Spirit," in which Linda's spirit visits him in the woods, in the form of a white squirrel. "You don't know if it's true. But it's a great thought. And it's an uplifting thought. So I allow myself to go there," McCartney said.

—InfoBeat

Souls who have passed on may send guidance when we urgently need it. *We need only listen.*

Communication is possible between those who live on this earth and those who live in a state of eternal repose, in heaven or purgatory. It may even be that God lets our loved ones send us messages to guide us at certain moments in our life.

—Rev. Gino Concetti
Chief Theological Commentator
L'Osservatore Romano, The Vatican

Medium-Facilitated Communications

Mediums are people who can communicate with the deceased. Many people seek out mediums to act as a go-between with the spirit world. Mediumship involves a cooperating effort between a live person on Earth and a deceased person. The medium uses clairvoyance to "see", clairaudience to "hear", and clairsentience to "feel" the spirit. What happens is a form of telepathy with the person in the spirit world.

Harry Edwards, a famous medium, compared the process to being akin to playing a violin.

Like a Violin

If the instrument is a poor one, it is reflected in the musical tones that come from it. The result also reflects the musician's intimacy and knowledge of how to use the violin. Give the master violinist a superb instrument, and the result is far different. Every good instrumentalist has to know his instrument, the feel of it, and this can only come through usage and experience. It is just the same with mediumship.

—Harry Edwards

We Are Always Connected

Mediums tell us that we are always telepathically connected to our departed loved ones. All we must do is to think about them and they feel us calling.

> You can communicate your love with departed loved ones in an instant—simply by calling them to memory and using the power of your thoughts to speak to them. Our loved ones hear us when we do that. They are as near as our next breath if we want them to be.
>
> —Char Margolis
> *Questions from Earth*
> *Answer from Heaven*

Children can see through the veils of spirit, especially if there is a need. Generally they retain this ability until they are embarrassed, put down, or made fun of during the early years of school.

> It's really important to understand that our loved ones feel our thoughts and good wishes. So many times I'll give clients a name and say, "Is it your grandmother?" And they'll say, "Yes—please tell her I love her." I reply, "You're the one who has the connection. Just feel the love for your grandmother and think, 'I love you.' And she'll know it. You don't need me to connect to someone you love."
>
> —Char Margolis

You must want to communicate with departed spirits and learn how to receive communication from them.

If you ever decide to have a session with a medium, think carefully. Think about who you want to come, examine your own motivation, and realize the souls have their own mind and their own way of helping. It may not be your way, but it is a way worth hearing. All the communication from the souls, no matter how insignificant to why we have come in the first place, is of vital importance to our journey here. They know a lot more than we do about life on earth, because they lived it to completion and gained the reward for a job well done.

—George Anderson

We Don't Die

I advise people to give it six months before you start to communicate, in order to let the other person get used to their life on the other side and you get used to your new life here.

—Echo Bodine

Echoes of the Soul

Messages from spirits are be subtle—a whisper, not a shout. You must be listening and receptive to hear them.

The next to thing to remember about spirit-communication is that if you are not listening, you won't hear. Those in spirit make every effort to get our attention in ways that are gentle and non-threatening, so much so that these subtle messages are often missed.

—Lori Lothian

Cues can include a ringing in the ears, a fleeting image of movement in our peripheral vision and of course, dream appearances and waking signs.

There are different ways our loved ones will try to communicate with us. For example, if we have their picture on the mantle they'll move the picture or try to tip it over. Maybe they'll come into the room and they'll have a scent on them like the smell of Old Spice which reminds you of Grandpa or a bunch of peonies like Grandma had in her garden ... and they will actually project that smell to us.

—Echo Bodine
Relax! It's Only a Ghost

Talking to Loved Ones
On the Other Side

Communicating with deceased souls can feel like talking to oneself inside your head. You can communicate by thinking the conversation or writing in a journal—especially if asking a question.

Communication is always a two-way street and it's no different when chatting with the dead. We can ask for guidance from the departed by simply thinking it or writing down our questions in a journal. Answers come through signs, synchronicities and sometimes dream conversations.

—Lori Lothian

Fear, guilt, shame. anger and other negative emotions get in the way of communing with loved ones who have transitioned from the physical world. Emotions that run deep often act as an unconscious barrier to making an afterlife connection and dealing with grief.

Talking to the dead is more like placing a long distance phone call to a third world country—the connection can be tenuous and static-filled, but in the end it is as simple as dialing. On the other hand, going to a medium to talk to dear departed grandma is like placing an operator-assisted call—you only need to resort to that more expensive option after your own attempts have failed.

—Lori Lothian

James Van Praagh is a survival-evidence medium, meaning that he is able to bridge the gap between that of the living and that of the dead, by providing evidential proof of life after death via detailed messages. He says the true essence of the messages are the feelings behind the words.

The spirits communicate by their emotions. No words exist in the English language, or any other for that matter, which can describe the intense sensations.

—James Van Praagh

Often the first thing that those close to death experience is the realization that there are friendly spirits in the room, who arrive with the express purpose of carrying them to another realm.

—Dr. Peter Fenwick

9

VISITATIONS

Deathbed visions (DBV) are visions a dying person may have in the minutes, hours, or days before his or her death. In contrast, near-death experiences are experiences that occur to an ill or injured person who recovers and doesn't die at that time.

As death approaches, a dying person may see deceased loved ones who offer support and guidance in their transition. Hospice and health care workers say they know death is eminent when the person has a deathbed vision.

A wife's description of her husband's death: "The gauze over his face moved, I ran to him and with his last strength he said to me: 'Adrianna, my dear, your mother—who had died three years before—is helping me break out of this disgusting body. There is so much light here, so much peace.'

—Paola Giovetti

As Old As Mankind

Instances of death-bed visions have been recorded throughout history.

The phenomenon of deathbed visions is as old as humankind, and such visitations of angels, light beings, previously deceased personalities and holy figures manifesting to those about to cross over to the Other Side have been recorded throughout all of human history.

—Brad Steiger

Many believe that death-bed visions stand as one of the most compelling proofs of life after death.

The evidence of Visions of the Dying, when they appear to see and recognize some of their relatives of whose decease they were unaware affords perhaps one of the strongest arguments in favour of survival.

—Sir William Barrett

Skeptics say deathbed visions they are hallucinations induced by drugs, fever, disease, oxygen deprivation, wish fulfillment, and depersonalization. However, in most cases hallucinations arising from these factors generally concern the present and not the afterworld.

Most dying persons having death-bed visions were not on medications and were coherent up to the moment of death. Sedation, high fever, and painkilling drugs seems to decrease, rather than to increase ability to experience these phenomena.

Trends in line with the survival hypothesis occurred predominantly in patients whose mentality was not disturbed by sedatives or other medications, who had no diagnosed hallucinogenic pathology, and who were fully conscious as well as responsive to their environment.

—Dr. Karlis Osis

Family members and hospital personnel report that dying relatives, who had been weak or even comatose, may suddenly sit up moments before the last breath— seemingly revived, to stare at a corner of the room and call out the name of a deceased loved one.

The dying person usually sees or hears friends or relatives who have already passed over.

In general, the people who are waiting for us on the other side are the ones who loved us the most. You always meet those people first.

—Elizabeth Kubler-Ross

Sometimes the visitation is someone the dying person does not know has already died.

Peter was staring intently at the foot of his bed and he suddenly regained his energy and then started talking to an invisible presence. When his family arrived, he told them that he'd been visited by his sister in the night and that they'd had a long chat. The strange thing was, his sister had died the week before, but nobody had dared tell him because they thought the shock might kill him. There was absolutely no way he could have known about his sister's death. It was in that moment that I realized Peter was going to die, no matter how much medical attention he received. When a patient says that they have been 'visited' by a dead loved one, you know that their time has come. It's commonly accepted by nurses and we see it quite a lot.

—Dr. Penny Sartori RGN, PhD
Morriston Hospital in Swansea

5keptics argue that the visions are caused by altera-
tions in brain chemistry. But this doesn't explain how
dying people sometimes "see" someone he or she didn't
know had died.

Two little girls, Jennie and Edith, contracted diphtheria. On
Wednesday, Jennie died but her death was kept from Edith. On
Saturday, Edith felt she was dying and asked that two of her photographs be sent to Jennie along with her farewell. Just before her
death at 6:30 that evening, she "saw" several friends she knew to
be dead and then exclaimed, "Why, papa! Why, papa! You did not
tell me Jennie was here! . . . O, Jennie, I'm so glad you are here!"
—James Hyslop

A relative or friend may have a visitation from a dying person at the moment of their death. They may be
awakened from a deep sleep by a feeling or even by a vision of the dying loved one. Often a phone call confirming death comes minutes later.

The moment my mother passed in the hospital, I awoke at
home early in the morning, and knew she was no longer
"here" on this plane of existence. Ten minutes later the
phone rang. It was a call from a family friend confirming
what I already knew in my heart.
—Carla Wills-Brandon
One Last Hug Before I Go

Commonly a person who has recently died will visit close friends and relatives as if to announce their death.

A very large number of apparition cases involve a person who has recently died appearing to one or more loved ones to announce the fact of their death. In many such cases the death was unexpected and was later confirmed to have occurred immediately before the apparition.

—Victor Zammit

Deathbed visions may be accompanied by odd events in the environment immediately around the dying person. Clocks may stop working, paintings may fall off the wall, or gusts of wind may sweep through the room.

Collective Viewings

Dr. Osis's research found cases in which those who had gathered around the patient's deathbed all saw the vision. There were numerous instances of "extrasensory" interaction between patients and attending physicians and nurses.

Dr. Karlis Osis of the American Society for Psychical Research interviewed more than 640 doctors and nurses who attended an average of 50 - 60 dying people—totally over 35,000 cases. He reported a number of fascinating consistencies in these mysterious visions:

- ♦Most visions are of familiar people who have previously passed away;

- ♦Usually the friends and relatives seen in the visions say they have come to help take them away.

- ♦The dying person is unafraid and reassured, expressing happiness;

- ♦The dying person's mood—even state of health— seems to change from depressed or pain-riddled to elation and momentarily relieved of pain until death strikes.

- ♦Experiencers are aware of their real surroundings and conditions and do not seem to be hallucinating;

- ♦Belief or disbelieve in an afterlife doesn't seem to be a factor.

—Dr. Karlis Osis
At the Hour of Death

Help Comes

Kubler-Ross found that when a patient died, someone was always there to help in the transition from
life to death, often a deceased family member or friend.
Those who had experienced a "comeback" from death to
life assured her that to die was to experience a feeling
of "peace, freedom, equanimity, a sense of wholeness,"
and said they were no longer afraid to die.

No One Dies Alone

Most deathbed visions are of light beings that may be
dead persons known to the dying, or great religious or
mythical figures, such as the Virgin Mary, Jesus, and so
on. Regardless of racial, cultural, religious, educational,
age, and socioeconomic lines the visions have common
characteristics, such as radiant lights, scenes of majes-
tic beauty, beings of light, and feelings of serene peace.
Generally their appearance elicits a response of joy,
peace, happiness, and cessation of pain.

Fear and Anxiety Eases

Visions include architectural structures, and symbolic transitional features like gates, bridges, rivers,
and boats. Afterworld scenes are populated with angels
and spirits of the dead. Reminiscent of the near-death
experience, celestial music may permeate the vision
and colors are vivid. Visions tend to conform to the dying person's religious expectations.

Visitation Prompted Kubler-Ross's Work

The turning point for Dr. Elisabeth Kubler-Ross in her work as a medical doctor occurred in a Chicago hospital in 1969 when a deceased patient appeared before her in fully materialized form. Kubler-Ross had been feeling discouraged about her research with the dying because of the opposition that she had encountered among her colleagues, but the apparition of Mary Schwartz told her not to abandon her work because life after death was a reality.

Health professionals tending the dying and their loved ones tell stories of visitations.

Suddenly there was the most brilliant light shining from my husband's chest, and as this light lifted upward, there was the most beautiful music and singing voices. My own chest seemed filled with infinite joy, and my heart felt as if it was lifting to join this light and music. Suddenly, there was a hand on my shoulder, and a nurse said, "Sorry, love. He's just gone." I lost sight of the light and the music and felt so bereft at being left behind.

—*Account told to Dr. Peter Fenwick*

Apparitions

An apparition is a vision of the spirit of a decease person or animal, typically referred to as a ghost. Even though apparitions have been reported from the earliest times, they continue to be a mystery

- They can appear and disappear very suddenly.

- They can move through walls, cast shadows and their reflection can be seen in a mirror.

- They may appear solid or fuzzy or transparent. They often appear as a white haze.

- Those warning of danger cast a black shadow or appear as a black haze.

- They may be accompanied by smells or a sensation of chills.

- They seem to have a purpose such as communicating a message or giving comfort to the grieving.

Apparitions are often spontaneous.

Many [apparitions] occur, for example, while the percipient is in a relaxed state or concentrating on some activity like reading, or is performing routine work. In some instances the person may simply be tired, as from a long day's work. Under such conditions, particularly in the case of imaginative individuals, a mental image might be superimposed upon the visual scene to create a "sighting"

—Joe Nickell
Looking for a Miracle

Contrary to what we might expect, more highly-educated patients evidenced *more* deathbed phenomena than the less well-educated, thus contradicting the allegation that the more superstitious are likely to experience deathbed phenomena.

Deathbed visitations are often discounted as rantings of the infirm and crazy, or ignored completely. Dying individuals experiencing deathbed visions are often misdiagnosed, disregarded, ignored, heavily medicated or shut away.

Mirror Gazing Visitations

Gazing into a reflective medium, like a mirror or still water can sometimes stimulate a visitation. Also called *scrying*, the person relaxes into a meditative state and, in a dim light, gazes into the reflection in an out-of-focus manner. Amazing images appear, including those of people who have died—some of whom actually converse with the gazer.

> The great seer Nostradamus used a reflective device to see into the future.

Moody's Psychomanteum Chamber

Dr. Raymond Moody constructed a small room with a comfortable chair and large mirror, which he called a psychomanteum chamber to facilitate communication with dead people. Moody says it is a therapeutic tool to heal grief and bring insight. He reported research with 300 subjects in his book, *Reunions*.

The chamber is a dark room, about ten feet by ten feet, with a mirror on one wall and a light behind a chair that provides just enough brightness to see the mirror. Sitting in the chair, the experiencer gazes into the mirror. The experience may be a few minutes to as long as 2 or 3 hours. Some people experience something quickly, and others don't see anything at all.

how to call up a visitation

- *Food*: Eat fruit and vegetables. Avoid caffeine and dairy products the day before your encounter.

- *Location*: Select a comfortable, quiet place where you can truly relax and won't be disturbed. Turn off clocks and phones.

- *Clothing*: Wear loose, comfortable clothing. Take off shoes and jewerly, unbuckle belts.

- *Mirror*: Place a large mirror in front of comfortable chair so that you can gaze into it while holding your eyes at a comfortable angle.

- *Light*: Dim light from behind usually works the best. Experiment to find what works best for you. The twilight hours inspire altered states in many people.

- *Chair*: Sit in a comfortable chair that supports your head.

- *Posture*: Make sure that you are sitting comfortably.

- *Awareness*: Ease into an altered state of awareness by relaxing. Empty your mind. Breath slowly and deeply.

- *Mood*: Create a serene mood by playing soft music and looking at beautiful art.

- *Memories*: Look at favorite photos and personal items to bring fond memories of your loved ones to mind.

Mirror Gazing is Easy

*S*it comfortably, relax and gaze into the clear depth of the mirror without trying to see anything. Some compare this to looking off into the distance. Properly relaxed, your arms will feel very heavy and the tips of your fingers will tingle as though charged slightly by electricity. This tingling feeling almost always signals the beginning of the hypnagogic or altered state of consciousness.

Changes in the clarity of the mirror signals that visions are about to appear. Usually the mirror will become cloudy like the sky on a cloudy day; other times the mirror seems to darken.

Attempting to guide the images has an inhibiting effect. Instead,passively watch the visions unfold. It is best to wait until you become adept at seeing images in the reflection before putting questions for the vision.

Let Images Come

People report astounding experiences. Some see and have conversations with departed family and friends. Some even experience physical contact, such as a hug

Some of Dr. Moody's subjects maintained images for as long as ten minutes on their first attempt. Usually, however, they last several seconds, increasing in length with proficiency.

Every Visitation is Different

Some people experience sensations of a given person, or location, without actually seeing anything. Others may hear the departed person talk, or feel his or her touch. Sometimes, like Nostradamus, one will seem to pass into the mirror, or the image may actually come out to be with the gazer.

A man in Pennsylvania lost his favorite daughter in an accident. She had gone swimming at a lake with several friends and drowned.... Two days later, on the day of the burial service, the man was putting his tie on in front of the bathroom mirror when an apparition of the dead daughter suddenly appeared next to him. She was still dressed in her swinsuit and was soaking wet as though she had just been pulled out of the lake. She stood next to her father and put her hand on his shoulder. Then she kissed him on the cheek, said, "Good-bye," and disappeared....The man's other daughter insisted that his shoulder and the side of his face were wet when he came out of the bathroom and told his family of his remarkable experience.

—Raymond Moody, M.D.
Reunions
Visionary Encounters with Departed Loved Ones

WHEEL OF KARMA

WHAT GOES AROUND, COMES AROUND.

10

REINCARNATION

The concept of reincarnation offers one of the most attractive explanations of mankind's origin and destiny, and provides us with the opportunity to enhance our own spiritual and personal growth.

I am confident that there truly is such a thing as living again, that the living spring from the dead, and that the souls of the dead are in existence.

—Socrates

Reincarnation answers a lot of questions that non-reincarnation can't answer. Who we are, why we are in the situation we are in, what we should do about it, what we can learn from it, and where we are headed.

Were an Asiatic to ask me for a definition of Europe, I should be forced to answer him: It is that part of the world which is haunted by the incredible delusion that man was created out of nothing, and that his present birth is his first entrance into life.

—Arthur Schopenhauer

Generations come and generations go, but the earth remains forever. The sun rises and the sun sets, and hurries back to where it rises. The wind blows to the south and turns to the north; round and round it goes, ever returning on its course. All streams flow into the sea, yet the sea is never full. To the place the streams come from, there they return again...What has been will be again, what has been done will be done again; there is nothing new under the sun.

—Ecclesiastes 1:4-9

Giving consideration to the possibility of reincarnation may change the way you think about death.

Live so that thou mayest desire to live again—that is thy duty—for in any case thou wilt live again!

–Friedrich Nietzsche

To know that you lived many lives before this one and that there are many more to come is a attractive perspective from which to judge the meaning of this life.

All life changes its aspect when reincarnation becomes a settled conviction, beyond all argument, raised above all dispute. Each day of life is but one page in the great drama of existence; each sorrow but a fleeting shadow cast by a passing cloud; each joy but a gleam of sunshine reflected from a swinging mirror; each death but the moving from a worn-out house. The strength of an eternal youth begins slowly to pass into the awakening life; the calmness of a vast serenity broods over the tossing waves of human thought. The radiant glory of the immortal Intelligence pierces the thick dusky clouds of matter, and the imperishable Peace that nought can ruffle sheds its pure whiteness over the triumphant spirit.

—Annie Besan

For thirty years I have leaned toward the theory of Reincarnation. It seems a most reasonable philosophy and explains many things. No, I have no desire to know what, or who I was once; or what, or who, I shall be in the ages to come. This belief in immortality makes present living the more attractive. It gives you all the time there is. You will always be able to finish what you start. There is no fever or strain in such an outlook. We are here in life for one purpose—to get experience. We are all getting it, and we shall all use it somewhere.

—Henry Ford

Source of Comfort

Reincarnation can be a source of great comfort, especially for those who seek liberation on the basis of their inner resources. It gives assurance for continuing one's existence in further lives and thus having a renewed chance to attain liberation.

I cannot think of permanent enmity between man and man, and believing as I do in the theory of reincarnation, I live in the hope that if not in this birth, in some other birth I shall be able to hug all of humanity in friendly embrace.

—Mahatma Ghandi

Though I may not be a king in my future life, so much the better: I shall nevertheless live an active life and, on top of it, earn less ingratitude.

—Frederick the Great

We Create Our Future Life Experiences

Reincarnation is a way of rejecting the monotheistic teaching of the final judgment by a holy God, with the possible result of being eternally condemned to suffer in hell.

I can assure you that death is another beginning. You have lived before and you will live again, and when you are done with physical existence, you will still live. I want you to feel your own vitality. Feel it travel through the universe and know that it is not dependent upon your physical image.

—Seth

Many verified life histories can be more logically explained by the "general reincarnation hypothesis" than by other after-death theories. If it is real for people like the Dalai Lama, it is equally likely that you and all other humans are reincarnations of people who have lived before.

One Life Among Many Dreams

As we live through thousands of dreams in our present life, so is our present life only one of many thousands of such lives which we enter from the other more real life and then return after death. our life is but one of the dreams of that more real life, and so it is endlessly, until the very last one, the very real, the life of God.
                                                    —count Leo Tolstoy

Most of what you are today may have evolved from knowledge and experience gained in previous lifetimes.

We have all lived past lives. All of us will live future ones. What we do in *this* life will influence our lives to come as we evolve toward immortality.

—Brian Weiss, M.D.
Many Lives, Many Masters

General Reincarnation Hypothesis

What you do in this life—what you study in school, where you live and work, whom you marry, or not, how you spend your free time, who your friends are, and what you feel about it—may influence events in future lives.

I adopted the theory of reincarnation when I was 26. Genius is experience. Some seem to think that it is a gift or talent, but it is the fruit of long experience in many lives.

—Henry Ford

Much thought-provoking evidence suggests that your physical appearance, the way you think, how you react emotionally to life events, the way you interact with other people, and the creative activities and vocations you choose may be predisposed by the experiences of one or more humans who lived in the past. Even if you don't know who they were, you may find what appears to be their "soulprints" in the person you are today and the manner in which you live.

−Paul von Ward
The Soul Genom

Reincarnation is not limited to human life or to life on Earth.

y life with Grey Eagle was prior to my birth here but that doesn't mean that we were together here on this Earth together in a previous life. And I also think that we have one life and just many journeys, and this Earth plane is one of those journeys. I think that we can choose to come back here onto this Earth and do this all over again if we want to. And I think there are those that do. But I also don't want to disregard the fact that we can choose to go out into the universe, as the universe is vast. Let's not assume that the Earth is the only place that we can travel to and have experiences from. There are many many places. So a person can come back to this Earth if he so chooses in another form, in another being but it isn't our only option.

—Rosemary Altea
The Eagle and the Rose

People look for some sort of physical confirmation that this cycle of reincarnation indeed happens ...

...BECAUSE THERE iS NO REAL PROOF.

Evidence from Hypnotic Regression

Healers have used hypnosis—whether they called it that or not—for thousands of years to assist their patients in soothing anxiety, overcoming insomnia and managing pain.

Patients often have an experience of being someone else in another time.

Search for Bridey Murphy

In 1952, therapist Morey Bernstein regressed Ruth Simmons back past the point of her birth. Ruth began speaking with an Irish accent, said her name was Bridey Murphy, who lived in 19th century Belfast, and recalled many details of her life, including names of two grocers from whom she bought food, Mr. Farr and John Carrigan. A Belfast librarian found a city directory for 1865-1866 that listed both men as grocers.

Hypnosis is a relaxed state of focused concentration. Deeper levels of the subconscious can be accessed through hypnosis.

We go in and out of hypnosis many times a day, such as when driving and then realizing that we have been on automatic pilot or when drifting off into a daydream.

The subconscious is not limited by boundaries of space or time.

A man in a hypnotic state experiences being a World War II soldier in a past life. He remembers a name, a place and how he died. He tells his therapist that he is suffering from a deep pain in his chest. Later the therapist looks up old World War II military records to find that a soldier with the same name had died from a bullet wound to the chest. While not "proof" of reincarnation, most hypno-therapist have had similar experiences.

There are thousands, even millions of cases similar the man who relived being a soldier in WWII.

The most promising evidence bearing on reincarnation seems to come from the spontaneous cases, especially among children.

–Ian Stevenson

spontaneous Childhood memories

Young children often give descriptions of past relationships and relatives, which are confirmed through historical records.

A friend wrote me, "When my daughter was five, she told me a long story that included,' The wagon turned over. Going down the steep bank. And the horses died.' I told her, 'I don't think that ever happened.' And then she said, 'Yes it did! You were there!' A moment later she said, 'Oh, I remember. That was when I was the other girl. You weren't my Mommy then.'"

—Paul Von Ward
The Soul Genome

How Young Malou "Spooked" His Father

Malou's family had lived in the area for generations as farmers. On a walk one day when he was a little kid. He asked, "Dad, where are the two houses that used to be here? One had a porch that was coming down. What about the road, where did it go?" He explained, "There *was* a road right here, we used it with the wagons!" What spooked his father was that there used to be tow houses right where Malou said they were. Further, one of them had a porch that was falling down. AN old wagon road had been where Malou said it was, but had reverted to brush. His father kept repeating, "No way you would know that, you weren't even born yet!"

—Paul Von Ward
The Soul Genome

Von Ward researched numerous cases of people who fervently believe that they had been a particular person in the past. His book, *The Soul Genome,* he presents side-by-side photos, revealing the uncanny resemblance between the living person and the person they thought themselves to be in a past life. For example, a woman names Sherrie believes that she was Marilyn Monroe. The biometric analysis of photographs of their faces varied by only one percent, suggesting that they resembled one another more than either resembles anyone else.

Soul Families

We are psychically bound to the people closest to us and they will continue to be closest to us throughout our migratory journey, though they likely will not be in the same life role in each reincarnation, making them unrecognizable to us in our present everyday life.

We all seem to stay together with the same people that we felt close with—birds of a feather flock together. We may have different parents, our brother or sister could be our parent next time. But we do seem to stay with the same other souls that we feel a certain affinity with, or a good vibration with. This may explain why we feel closer with our sister than our brother, or why you feel we've always been together with the same people from the beginning, but maybe we meet different people along the line, who would highlight, enhance, or play an important role in our lives at that specific point.

—George Anderson
Afterlife Encounters

Friends are all souls that we've known in other lives. We're drawn to each other. Even if I have only known them a day, it doesn't matter. I'm not going to wait till I have known them for two years, because anyway, we must have met somewhere before, you know."

—George Harrison

These entities may include pets, friends, enemies, and any other individual who has touched our lives—positively or negatively.

I have been here before, but when or how I cannot tell:

I know the grass beyond the door,
The sweet keen smell, the sighing sound, the lights around the shore.

You have been mine before - How long ago I may not know:

But just when at that swallow's soar, your neck turned so,

Some veil did fall, - I knew it all of yore.

—Dante Gabriel Rossetti

Souls are poured from one into another of different kinds of bodies of the world.

—Jesus Christ
Pistis Sophia

Spiritual Recycling

Reincarnation is the cosmic vehicle for recycling life.

Reincarnation is essential to enable the soul to evolve to its Divine right.

—R.F. Goudey
Reincarnation
A Universal Truth

To be born here and to die here,
  to die here and to be born elsewhere,

To be born there and to die there,
  to die there and to be born elsewhere,

That is the round of existence.

—*Buddhist Text*

I'm a great believer in the hereafter, in karma, in reincarnation. It does make sense. I believe that God is not just a lawgiver, but a creative artist. The greatest of all. And what characterizes artists is that they want to redo their work. Maybe it didn't come off perfectly, so they want to see it done again, and improved. Reincarnation is a way for God to improve his earlier works.

—Norman Mailer

Instant Chemistry

Reincarnation may explain our instant attraction or rapport with certain people and instant dislike or distrust for others.

Religious View

Most religions tell of a migratory
journey of the soul after death.

> Christians, Hindus, and Buddhists
> all believe in the migratory process,
> though they approach it in very dif-
> ferent ways.

Buddhism

Mind or consciousness is the center of our
lives. We process everything though the filter of our
thoughts—consciousness. How we act reflects how we
think. We are peaceful when the mind is peaceful.

> *According
> to Buddhism
> our transition
> to our next life
> will be peaceful
> when the mind
> is peaceful.*

If we cultivated peace and kindness, we will be reborn in a peaceful world filled with loving beings. If, on the other hand, we are filled with anger and jealousy and hurt others, we will take rebirth in hellish worlds, for Buddhism teaches that there are many other worlds aside from the animal and human worlds that we see.

—Tulku Thondop Rinpoche

The Bardo

Buddhism says the mind exits the body as we lose consciousness when we die. In the *bardo*—the transitional passage between death and the next birth—we regain consciousness. Experience in the *bardo* is shaped by our habitual thoughts and feelings.

> The *bardo* is a mental projection—like dreaming.

Challenges in the Bardo

A *delog*, who was an accomplished yogi in life, was traversing a narrow mountain pass over a precipice in the *bardo* when he came to a massive rock wall. There was no way around the wall. Looking more closely he saw an opening about the size of his fist through which he could see to the other side. Musing at the smallness of the hole, he remembered: "Consciousness can get through anything," and instantly found himself on the other side of the wall.

Delogs are near-death experiencers—
people who have died and returned
to tell of their travels in the realm of
death.

Just as a people dreaming may not
be aware that they are dreaming during a
dream, we may not realized that we have
died and are in the *bardo*.

Because of having had a body when living *bardo* beings experience themselves as still being in a body.

But when they may try to speak to family and friends and they are ignored because no one sees them. Confused and upset, they may cry out, *"I'm not dead! I'm right here."*

Buddhism offers many meditations to prepare for death. Whatever we do, though, we need to practice beforehand. Right now, it is easy to change our mental habits, but hard to restructure our circumstances because we live within the strictures of a solid body and society. In the *bardo*, on the other hand, it is hard to change our mental habits, but easy to restructure our circumstances because at death our habits alone determine our world.

—Tulku Thondop Rinpoche

The Tibetan Book of the Dead describes in detail the experiences one has in the intermediary state between two incarnations, suggesting that the deceased keeps some personal attributes. Although it is not clear what actually survives after death in this case, it mentions a mental body that cannot be injured by the visions experienced by the deceased

When it happens that such a vision arises, do not be afraid! Do not feel terror! you have a mental body made of instincts; even if it is killed or dismembered, it cannot die! since in fact you are a natural form of voidness, anger at being injured is unnecessary! The yama Lords of Death are but arisen from the natural energy of your own awareness and really lack all substantiality. voidness cannot injure voidness!

—Tibetan Book of the Dead

Ancient Egypt

Egyptians believed that the soul transmigrated from body to body, which is why they preserved the bodies of their dead so that the body could make the journey along with the soul.

Resurrection

The Egyptian Book of the Dead describes the travel of the soul into the next world without making any allusions to its return to earth. The ancient Egyptians embalmed the dead in order that the body might be preserved and accompany the soul into that world. This suggests their belief in resurrection rather than in reincarnation.

New Age thinking sees reincarnation as an eternal progression of the soul toward higher levels of spiritual knowledge. Thus what reincarnates is not the impersonal *atman*, but an entity which is currently called the soul, an entity which preserves the attributes of personhood from one life to the next.

Karma

Through the law of karma, the effects of all deeds actively create past, present, and future experiences, thus making one responsible for one's own life, and the pain and joy it brings. The results or "fruits" of actions are called *karma-phala*. The concept can be traced back to the early Upanishads.

Karma extends through one's present life and all past and future lives as well.

All living creatures are responsible for their karma—their actions and the effects of their actions.

What goes around comes around.

According to the Upanishads and Vedanta philosophy, the entity that reincarnates is the impersonal self or *atman*.

The spiritual progress one accumulates toward realizing the *atman-Brahman* identity is recorded by karma, or rather by a minimal amount of karmic debt. The physical and mental complex of a human being is reconstructed at (re)birth according to one's karma. The newly shaped person experiences the fruits of actions from previous lives and has to do his or her best to stop the vicious cycle *avidya-karma-samsara*.

Explains Inequities & Accidents of Birth

Another major reason reincarnation is accepted by so many people today is that it seems to explain differences among people. Some are healthy, others are tormented their whole life by physical handicaps. Some are rich, others at the brink of starvation. Some have success without being religious; others are constant losers, despite their religious dedication.

Eastern religions explain these differences as a result of previous lives, good or bad, which bear their fruits in the present one through the action of karma. Therefore reincarnation seems to be a perfect way of punishing or rewarding one's deeds, without the need of accepting a personal God as Ultimate Reality.

I believe past experiences are not necessarily punishments form the past, or even lessons or patterns carried forward from past lives. By choosing to come into a particular family or constellation of circumstances you have not agreed to submit to abuse. However, you have agreed to participate in how a certain lesson or teaching is carries out and so do the other individuals who have chosen to share the lifetime with you. Just because you have agreed to play a role in this family, abuse is not the invariable result. Part of the learning process is learning *not* to choose the more harmful or destructive paths.

—Brian Weiss

Through Time into Healing

Death has such great importance in this society that it affects everything. I learned from my guru that death is not the enemy, I see it as another moment. Yet it's the end of an incarnation and means going on to another incarnation.

—Ram Dass

I did not begin when I was born, nor when I was conceived. I have been growing, developing, through incalculable myriads of millenniums. All my previous selves have their voices, echoes, promptings in me. Oh, incalculable times again shall I be born.

—Jack London

Remote viewing proves that the mind can reach out beyond the physical body.

11

REMOTE VIEWING

If consciousness can exist outside of the physical body—i.e., outside of the brain—then it is easier to suppose that consciousness continues after death. Remote viewing (RV) provides some of the most persuasive evidence that consciousness can reach out from the body.

> There's more to us than
> just inhabiting a physical body.
> —Russell Targ
> *Limitless Mind*

Remote viewing is a mental faculty that enables a "viewer" to give details about a target that is inaccessible to normal senses due to being at a distance, in another time, or otherwise out of view. Viewers can describe locations on the other side of the world that they have never visited; they can describe events from the past, objects inside containers or locked in a room all without being told anything about the target.

What makes remote viewing so persuasive is that it was developed by Stanford Research Institute physicists, Russell Targ and Harold Puthoff. After being introduced to the process in the early 1970s by Inga Swann, a psychic, who coined the term remote viewing, Targ and Puthoff began using scientific protocol to study the phenomena.

As scientists we consider it important to examine various models describing the operation of these effects so that we can determine the relationship between extraordinary human functioning and the physical and psychological laws we presently understand. It is not the purpose of our work at the SRI to add to the literature another demonstration of the statistical appearance of these phenomena in the laboratory, but rather we seek to achieve an understanding more compatible with contemporary science, and more useful to mankind.

—Harold Puthoff
Mind-Reach

Puthoff and Targ employed scientific protocol to test the effectiveness of remote viewing.

Targets Selected

A hundred sites within 30 minute drive from Menlo Park, California, such as buildings, bridges, playgrounds, were selected for the target pool and assigned a random number, placed in sealed envelopes, and stored in a safe.

Experiments

Each experiment consisted of a viewer, an interviewer and an outbounder. The outbounder threw a nine-sided die to select an envelope containing a target and then drove to the target site. At an agreed upon time the interviewer back in the lab, turned on the tape recorder and told the viewer to describe the target—the location in the envelope to where the outbounder had traveled.

Viewing

Viewers drew pictures of impressions and their verbal responses to the interviewer's questions about the target were recorded.

Feedback

The final step was for the viewer, the interviewer and the outbounder to all go to the target site so that the viewer would get feedback on his or her viewing accuracy.

Results were "statistically significant", meaning that they were not likely to have been caused by chance—something was going on!

We were surprised at the accuracy. In one case where the target was a swimming pool, the viewer actually described the dimensions to within 10% of its physical size.

-Russell Targ
Mind Reach

Puthoff and Targ had tapped into something very interesting.

Anyone Can Do It!

The ability to remote view is not limited to a few natural psychics. It is an innate ability that all humans possess. It is like studying a musical instrument or learning to draw, we all have some capability to acquire the techniques and put them into practice. Virtually anyone can remote view but, aw with language or dancing, it is skill that must be learned and practiced, to be effective.

L iterally thousands of experiments have shown that almost everyone can do this, and that viewers are able to describe with all their senses what they are perceiving. Remote Viewing is a little understood but fully normal ability. There is nothing supernatural going on, no spirits are involved, nor will being able to do it raise your IQ, although there is some evidence it will awaken your intuitive abilities, and possibly leave you more creative. Remote Viewing should not be confused with enlightenment.

—Stephan A. Schwartz

We all have some remote viewing ability and it can be developed from innate intuitive "muscles" we already possess. This suggests that there is universal knowledge that human consciousness is capable of taping into. But does it indicate that the mind can reach beyond the physical body? If the mind can do that, then can the mind survive the death of the body?

As far as we can tell, the ability to access nonlocal awareness, to open to that aspect of our consciousness that seems to operate outside the bounds of time and space, is spread throughout the population in a bell curve—much like any other human skill such as learning music.

—Stephan A. Schwartz

The remote viewing research was so interesting that it caught the attention of the CIA and U.S. Army who spent millions of taxpayers' dollars over twenty years on the highly classified covert spying program called Stargate. The program involved using psychics for such operations as finding Gaddafi of Libya (so our Air Force could drop bombs on him) and the locating of a missing airplane in Africa.

δumbo's feather

In the animated Disney movie, a baby elephant with huge ears believes he can fly only when he is clutching in his trunk a magic feather. In the end, he discovers the feather is only a crutch, without which he can still fly perfectly well. Just like Dumbo's feather, crystal balls and tarot cards and other accessories to the paranormal may be nothing more than psychological crutches, while remote viewing may turn out to be the expression of a human perception that transcends normal physical constraints on the senses without the need for artifacts. There is more to learn before we know for sure.

—Paul H. Smith
Reading the Enemy's Mind

Remote viewing is an attention management skill. Information not available to the ordinary physical senses comes in the form of words and mental images.

But how does remote viewing work?

Instead of signals being sent, the data suggest that the desired information is always present and available.

The remote viewer's focused intention "calls forth" the information.

Repository of All Information

Theosophists believe that "The Akashic Records" contain a compendium of mystical knowledge encoded in a non-physical plane of existence.

These records contain all knowledge of human experience and the history of the cosmos. They are metaphorically described as a library and other analogues commonly found in discourse on the subject include a universal computer, the Mind of God, and The Matrix.

The Matrix

The Matrix is an archive in the fullest sense: indifferent, dispassionate, with no capacity for judging; just data, pure and simple. Yes, it catalogues human acts and events. But all other facts about the universe are to be found there, as well; information about animate and inanimate objects; about places, landscapes, substances, emotions, physical and nonphysical qualities, artifacts, relations, things that are tangible and intangible, machines, history, personalities, everything....

Getting information from the Matrix rather than from the target itself allows a remote viewer to access anything about a target site, whether it involves past, present, or (to some degree) future; inside, outside, intangible or tangible, all regardless of what the target's condition or circumstances may be at the instant of the actual remote viewing.

—Paul H. Smith
Reading the Enemy's Mind

The **Matrix** or **Akashic Records** is a universal filing system which records every occurring thought, word, and action. The records, which are constantly undated, have been called the cosmic mind, the universal mind, the collective unconscious, and the collective subconscious.

> Carl Jung taught that each person's unconscious mind is connected to larger system –like a library with all thoughts and information in it—a matrix.

The essential features of the implicate order are that the whole universe is in some way enfolded in everything, and that each thing is enfolded in the whole.

—David Bohn, Physicist
The Undivided Universe

American mystic Edgar Cayce successfully read the Akashic Records in a sleep state or trance. Adherents believe that all phenomenal experience as well as transcendental knowledge is encoded in the Akashic Records.

We can see that the idea of an ancient record, a code, accessible to human anywhere if they are of the right frame of mind and heart is an old and cherished idea.
—Schwartz and Russek
The Living Energy Universe

LiKe a RaDio BRoaDcast

Veteran remote viewers say there is a remote viewing signal line that can be imprinted with selected data from the Matrix and which can carry this data to our individual minds.

It is like superimposing a complex waveform onto the carrier wave of a radio broadcast. The carrier wave provides the energy necessary to transport the signal over many miles. The information placed on the wave is communicated through the variations or fluctuations in the strength or shape of the wave. These fluctuations are a sort of code.

With a radio wave we need a radio receiver to catch the carrier wave and the coded information that the wave carries. For remote viewing, the "decoding" process is human consciousness.

It is quite possible that we humans may be "on-line" with the Matrix more often than we suppose, perhaps all the time. But because the results of this contact normally stay in the subconscious, we are seldom, if ever, consciously aware of it. The goal of remote viewing is to get the subconscious to loosen its grip on some of this hoard of data so we can do something useful with it.
—Paul H. Smith
Reading the Enemy's Mind

Like a hologram, each region of space-time contains information about every other point in space-time.

Information needs a medium to support it. It may be that at the quantum level information is transferred directly through some ethereal attachment point shared by everything in the universe. Or maybe it is passed via a quantum-level, non-local process similar to the mysterious way in which widely separated particles can be instantaneously affected by some influence at the subatomic level. But perhaps that's not how it works at all; maybe there is no universal point of connection, and maybe non-locality is incapable of transferring the large-scale information produced in remote viewing. We only know one thing for sure about whatever the mechanism might be; that remote viewing works, and so there must be *some* source for the information.

—Paul H. Smith
Reading the Enemy's Mind

Religion and Science Agree

... Separation is an illusion!

Hinduism teaches that individual consciousness (*Atman*) and universal consciousness (*Brahman*) are one.

> Quantum Physics tells us that we live in a "nonlocal" reality, which is to say that we can be affected by events that are distant from our ordinary awareness.

The parallel universes interpretation is one of the strangest ideas put forward by modern science. It could be also one of the most important in enabling us to understand not only how our brains work, but also lead to new forms of technology that would have far reaching implications to understanding the nature of human consciousness. If the parallel universes interpretation turns out to be correct and testable, our minds are capable of "tuning" to other parallel realities.

—Fred Alan Wolf
Dr. Quantum

The SRI remote viewing experiments showed that the viewer is not bound by present time. A viewer can focus attention at a specific location anywhere on—or off—the planet and describe what is there. In contemporary physics, we call this ability to focus attention on distant points in space-time "*nonlocal awareness*".

Remote viewing is an example of nonlocal ability. It has repeatedly allowed people to describe, draw, and experience objects and activities on the planet, contemporaneously or in the near future. Although we do not yet know how this works, there should no longer be any doubt that most of us are capable of experiencing places and events that appear to be separated from our physical bodies by space and time.

—Russell Targ
Limitless Mind

Data from dream research also provide convincing evidence that our minds have access to events occurring in distant places—even into the future.

If our minds—consciousness—can reach out thousands of miles to "view" remote sights, then consciousness must be able to exist and function outside of the body. And if it can do this, then it may be able to survive death.

When I look through my telescope at the spinning planets, I
can hear God's voice in the music of the spheres.

—Galileo

12

INTELLIGENT DESIGN

There are two schools of thought about the origins of the universe. One is called the "chance universe"; the other is the "intelligent design universe".

Chance Universe

According to neo-Darwinism, wholly undirected processes such as natural selection and random mutations are fully capable of producing the intricate designed-like structures in living systems. In their view, natural selection can mimic the powers of a designing intelligence without itself being directed by an intelligence.

Contradiction

A system is a set of interacting or interdependent entities, real or abstract, forming an integrated whole. If the entities making up the system are interdependent, then they cannot be random, because randomness presupposes complete independence.

...If everything in the universe is ultimately inter-connected and functions as layers and layers of systems, then the very conditions that define how randomness can occur are not present, and there-fore randomness is predicted not to be present.

—Schwartz and Russek
The Living Energy Universe

Natural selection out of chance mutations shapes what exists, but it cannot *create* anything new.

Natural selection is not a creative force in the sense that it stimulates novelty; it can only act on variations that have come into existence spontaneously, and independently of con-text. This is not to deny the potential power of natural selection to mold populations under certain circumstances; but there is an argument to be made that all useful novelties — indeed, any novelties at all — have to arise not as adaptations but as exaptations: in the broad sense, as features not acquired in the context of the function to which they will eventually be put.

—Ian Tattersall, Anthropologist
American Museum of Natural History

Intelligent Design Universe

Intelligent Design (ID) is the assertion that discoveries in quantum physics, cosmology, biochemistry, genetics, and paleontology question that chance *alone* can account for the intricate designed-like structures in the natural world and propose that *intelligence must be at work*.

Once you fully accept that the existence of ubiquitous order in the universe does not and cannot occur by chance—you are led inexorably to consider the possible existence of some sort of universal, invisible, intelligent Guiding-Organizing-Designing field process in the universe.

—Gary E. Schwartz
The G.O.D. Experiments

Intelligent causes can do things which undirected natural causes cannot.

Undirected natural causes can place scrabble pieces on a board, but cannot arrange the pieces as meaningful words or sentences.

Obtaining a meaningful arrangement requires an intelligent cause.

Logic is a very elegant tool and we've got a lot of mileage out of it for two thousand years or so. The trouble is, you know, when you apply it to crabs and porpoises, and butterflies and habit formation ... logic won't quite do ... because that whole fabric of living things is not put together by logic. You see when you get circular trains of causation, as you always do in the living world, the use of logic will make you walk into paradoxes.

—Gregory Bateson
to Fritjof Capra
Uncommon Wisdom

Intelligent Design presupposes neither a creator nor miracles. Intelligent Design is theologically minimalist. It detects intelligence without speculating about the nature of the intelligence.

There is only one type of cause that produces irreducibly complex systems, namely, "intelligence". Indeed, designing engineers played a role in the creation of all irreducibly complex systems—like an integrated circuit or internal combustion engine.

DNA is like a computer program, but far, far more advanced than any software we've ever created.

–Bill Gates

Evidence-Based Theory

Intelligent design is an evidence-based scientific theory about life's origins that challenges strictly materialistic views of evolution. It is not a religious-based belief. Intelligent design theory is supported by scientists, researchers and theorists at universities, colleges, and research institutes around the world.

Invisible Fields

The existence of dynamic invisible fields provides a plausible means by which a universal designing process could potentially orchestrate infinitely complex unfolding plans and designs.

> ... the most plausible alternative explanation for the incontrovertible evidence of the existence of complex and evolving orders in nature and the universe—whether the process is small or large, visible or invisible—is the process of what I have come to call the Guiding-Organizing-Designing process. *In the language of physics, this implies the existence of a universal "field"—including gravitational and magnetic fields—that functions as a formative process and provides intelligent guidance, organization, and creative design.*
>
> —Gary E. Schwartz
> *The G.O.D. Experiments*

Invisible fields include gravity, electro-magnetism, quantum, and other powerful but invisible forces.

Much of the mystery of our universe is created by invisible fields, which cannot be directly experienced through our five senses. No one has ever seen a gravitational field or ever measured one. We cannot measure gravity directly. What we do is observe objects and measurements, then *infer* the existence of an invisible force that cannot be seen or heard.

The physical brain is not needed for consciousness to survive.

When science combines this evolving body of experimental research with contemporary laboratory research on the topic of survival of consciousness after physical death, we discover compelling evidence that leads to a notable conclusion: that the brain is not required for conscious experience, intention, and intelligence.

—Gary E. Schwartz
The G.O.D. Experiments

Holonomic Brain Theory

Holonomic brain theory is a new model of human brain cognition developed by Stanford psychologist Karl Pribram with physicist David Bohm, that theorizes that memory/information is stored not in cells, but rather by a matrix of neurological wave interference patterns situated temporally between holographic Gestalt perception and discrete, affective, quantum vectors derived from reward anticipation potentials.

The Brain is a Hologram

Bohm's theory of the enfolding-unfolding-enfolding implicit order of the universe, states that our brains are smaller pieces of the larger hologram. That our brains contain the whole knowledge of the universe.

Pribram believes the brain is itself a hologram. Memories are encoded not in neurons, or small groupings of neurons, but in patterns of nerve impulses that crisscross the entire brain in the same way that patterns of laser light interference crisscross the entire area of a piece of film containing a holographic image.

A hologram produces an image that changes appearance as the viewer changes viewing angle. Each piece of the hologram contains some information about the entire image. This may explain how the brain encodes memories.

The Whole Is In Each Part

One of the most interesting qualities of the hologram is that the whole contains the knowledge of each part, and that each part contains the knowledge of the whole. If you break a hologram into many pieces each piece will still contain the whole image, but with a limited perspective. The image stays the same size but you lose clarity and you lose perspectives.

The "whole in every part" nature of a hologram provides us with an entirely new way of understanding organization and order.

Assume systems science predicts that what we are calling the G.O.D. (Guiding, Organizing Designing) process is the macro system. Then according to contemporary physics, all people would be intimately connected with the macro system (that is, "God") to varying degrees. The logic comes from basic physics. All physical objects—from atoms and chemicals, through organisms and planets, including solar systems and galaxies—are interconnected in various degrees by electromagnetic fields (as well as gravitational fields). Since all this information—interconnected and communicated by invisible fields—is circulating throughout the universe, we are all to some extent sharing the same information. This is a simple way to understand what is sometimes called the holographic universe.

—Gary E. Schwartz
The G.O.D. Experiments

Pribram's theory explains how the human brain can store so many memories in so little space.

The human brain has the capacity to memorize some 10 billion bits of information during the average human lifetime—about the same amount of information contained in five sets of the Encyclopedia Britannica.

Hologram theory explains our ability to quickly retrieve whatever information we need from the enormous store of our memories. In the human thinking process every piece of information seems to be cross-correlated with every other piece of information—another feature intrinsic to the hologram.

Researchers have discovered, for instance, that our visual systems are sensitive to sound frequencies, that our sense of smell is in part dependent on what are now called "osmic frequencies", and that even the cells in our bodies are sensitive to a broad range of frequencies. Such findings suggest that it is only in the holographic domain of consciousness that such frequencies are sorted out and divided up into conventional perceptions.

Matrix of Reality

The Quantum Hologram is, in the most fundamental sense, the matrix of our reality. It not only provides a first hand visual experience, but also a background, complete with our perceptions of time, dimension and the laws of the physical world. It's a construct of "reality", a combination of physical laws, common perceptions and an underlying collective unconscious.

—James Wallace

It's All An Illusion

As the religions of the East have long upheld, the material world is Maya, an illusion.

Tho we may think we are physical beings moving through a physical world, this too is an illusion.

We are really "receivers" floating through a kaleidoscopic sea of frequency, and what we extract from this sea and transmogrify into physical reality is but one channel from many extracted out of the superhologram.

—Michael Talbot
The Amazing Holographic Universe

Window to the Universe

Each mind has a limited perspective of the universal hologram. Our brains are our windows of perception. Each mind always contains the whole picture, but with a limited and unclear perspective. We each have different experience in our lives, but each perspective is valid.

All things in the universe are infinitely interconnected.

The SuperHologram is the Matrix

The superhologram is the matrix—it contains every subatomic particle that has been or will be—every configuration of matter and energy that is possible, from snowflakes to quasars, from whales to gamma rays

To see a World in a
Grain of Sand

And a Heaven in a Wild
Flower,

Hold Infinity in the palm
of your hand

And Eternity in an hour.

—William Blake
Auguries of Innocence

Accessing the SuperHologram

In a universe in which individual brains are actually indivisible portions of the greater hologram and everything is infinitely interconnected, remote viewing, telepathy, clairvoyance may merely be the accessing the holographic level.

I f the mind is actually part of a continuum, a labyrinth that is connected not only to every other mind that exists or has existed, but to every atom, organism, and region in the vastness of space and time itself, the fact that it is able to occasionally make forays into the labyrinth and have transpersonal experiences no longer seems so strange.

—Stanislav Grof, MD
The Holotropic Mind

Spiritual experiences are compatible with quantum physics explanations.

> If the rules of quantum mechanics apply all the way through to our psychological processes to what's going on in the nervous system—then we have an explanation perhaps, certainly we have a parallel, to the kind of experiences that people have called spiritual experiences. Because the *descriptions you get with spiritual experiences seem to parallel the descriptions of quantum physics.*
> —Karl Pribram
> Interview by Jeffrey Mishlove

If you were to run your hand through a hologram you would discover that there is nothing inside the projected image.

What we perceive as reality is only a canvas waiting for us to draw upon it any picture we want. Anything is possible, from bending spoons with the power of the mind to the phantasmagoric events experienced by Castaneda during his encounters with the Yaqui brujo don Juan, for magic is our birthright, no more or less miraculous than our ability to compute the reality we want when we are in our dreams.

—Michael Talbot
The Amazing Holographic Universe

In a holographic universe there are no limits to the extent to which we can alter the fabric of reality.

At its deeper level reality is a sort of superhologram in which the past, present, and future all exist simultaneously.

-Michael Talbot
The Amazing Holographic Universe

There is for me powerful evidence that there is something going on behind it all... It seems as though somebody has fine-tuned nature's numbers to make the Universe... The impression of design is overwhelming.

—Paul Davies

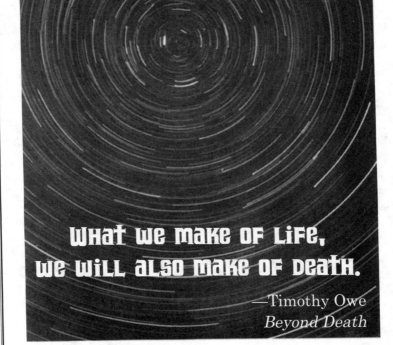

**WHAT WE MAKE OF LIFE,
WE WILL ALSO MAKE OF DEATH.**

—Timothy Owe
Beyond Death

13

BEYOND DEATH

C an the mind exist outside of the physical brain? If it cannot, then it is unlikely that there can be any existence after death. Instead, we simply cease to exist—oblivion. If, on the other hand, the mind—consciousness—*can* exist—and function—outside of the physical brain, *then* there is reason to believe in the possibility of an afterlife. What exactly that afterlife may be like is open for speculation. The possibilities are unlimited.

Some will argue that the mind resides in the brain because that is where some believe we store all the information we know. However, as a remote viewer, I will categorically state that is not necessarily true. I collect, analyze, and report information every day that I have never read, seen, or known prior to the experiment. It would seem that my mind is collecting it from somewhere. The mass of cerebral cells between my ears is the last place I think I would be looking for that information. No. . .there is a *somewhere-else,* and our minds not only have access to it, but may in fact at least partially reside within it. How large that place is or what else is there is up for question. So there is at least one other place besides physically reality, and my mind has access to it. Through extrapolation, one could say that *there is at least a physical world as well as a non-physical world.*

—Joseph McMoneagle
Mind Trek

Indeed, there is much to suggest that consciousness *can* exist outside of the physical brain. The most persuasive data comes from remote viewing research, which has yielded significant data supporting the mind's ability to reach out from the physical body to perceive.

Science has failed us when it comes to exploring the Afterlife

Science is inherently skeptical because science can only "disprove" a hypothesis. Empirical research always frames the question being explored as a "null" hypothesis, i.e., nothing is going on here. Then the researchers set out to "disprove" the null hypothesis.

Suppose researchers were studying differences between girls and boys. The null hypothesis would state that there is no difference between the sexes on the variable in question. Then the scientists would gather data, analyze it statistically to determine if there is a difference between the two groups, and if a difference is found, if it could it have been caused by chance.

If the difference is determined to be "significant", that means that the probability that the difference found is a chance occurrence is five in one hundred, which would be "significant at the .05 level"—the lowest acceptable level—to one in one thousand—the .001 level—which would mean that the probability that the result would occur by chance once in one thousand.

It is important to remind ourselves that science never "proves" anything; it only "disproves" and "improves" existing theories.

—Stanislav Grof, M.D.
The Holotropic Mind

SCIENCE CANNOT "PROVE" THAT THERE IS AN AFTERLIFE.
IT CAN ONLY DISPROVE THAT DEATH IS FINAL.

If you wish to upset the law that all crows are black it is enough if you prove one single crow to be white.
—William James

Using the "white crow" standard, near-death experiences—where people are declared clinically dead and then are revived to tell of incredible experiences—should disprove that death is final. But skeptics discount that near-death experiences prove that death is not final with the assertion that the person was not *actually* dead—as evidenced by their resuscitation—a rather circular argument!

No matter how reliable the evidence one might produce, if it flies in the face of the reigning paradigm, it will never be enough.

—Timothy Owe
Beyond Death

We are reluctant—especially the scientists and skeptics among us—to challenge our rooted beliefs. So just as when Galileo said that the Sun does not revolve around Earth, he was ridiculed and prosecuted.

A host of observed, but very basic human phenomena, including consciousness itself, have eluded rigorous scientific description by all disciplines of science. This is true, not because of insufficient evidence for a particular phenomenon's existence, but rather for lack of a theoretical construct, which could fit within the prevailing paradigms of science. For millennia philosophers have pondered the nature of mind, consciousness and mind/matter interactions but without sufficient knowledge and technical capability to propose properly testable theories.

—Edgar Mitchell
Apollo 14 Astronaut

We are stuck in the Newtonian view of the universe. We need a new paradigm that encompasses consciousness, spirit, the soul and eternity.

We hardly know how to deal with an abstract world such as envisioned by Plato or quantum physics. We've been more or less trained to look for things that can be grasped—things that are physical and solid. But the soul is not tangible, physical or solid. It doesn't even belong to you. It's more that you belong to it. You cannot just reach out and touch the soul. Yet, according to quantum physics principles and Plato's vision, the soul as an animating principle in the universe is ultimately more important than anything that is physical or tangible.

—Fred Alan Wolf
Dr. Quantum

Principles of quantum physics have opened up a new world of explanations and discovery. But the quantum universe is so different from our familiar Newtonian world, that we hardly know how to proceed.

Everything you've learned in school as "obvious" becomes less and less obvious as you begin to study the universe. For example, there are no solids in the universe. There's not even a suggestion of a solid. There are no absolute continuums. There are no surfaces. There are no straight lines.

—R. Buckminster Fuller

Many processes certainly *appear* to be explainable in approximately mechanistic reductionistic terms. But as physicists have delved progressively deeper into the nature of reality, they find that it cannot be understood in mechanistic terms. Mechanism assumes that there are separate objects that interact in determined, causal ways. But that's not the reality we live in. Quantum reality is holistic, and as such any attempt to study its individual pieces will give an incomplete picture.

—Dean Radin
Entangled Minds

Nature's Mind

What is the source of intelligent design? If not God, can it be Nature's Mind?

The fact that non-local correlations and non-local quantum information can now be seen as ubiquitous in nature leads to the conclusions that the quantum hologram can properly be labeled as "nature's mind" and that the intuitive function we label in humans as the "sixth sense" should properly be called the "first sense". The perception of non-local information certainly preceded and helped to shape, through learning feedback, the sensory systems that evolved in planetary environments, and which we currently label as the five normal senses.

We must conclude that evolved, complex organisms, which can form an intent and can produce and often do produce non-local causal effects associated with that intent. Further, that attention alone produces coherence in nature that in some measure reduces randomness.

—Edgar Mitchell
Apollo 14 Astronaut

The universe is consciousness, not physical matter.

We know that solid "things" are largely space. Where is the matter? It is something that we create in our minds with consciousness.

Our brains mathematically construct objective internal link-reality by interpreting internal link-frequencies that are ultimately projections from another internal link-dimension, a deeper order of existence that is beyond both space and time: The brain is a hologram folded in a holographic universe.

For Pribram, this synthesis made him realize that the objective world does not exist, at least not in the way we are accustomed to believing. What is "out there" is a vast ocean of internal link-waves and frequencies, and reality looks concrete to us only because our brains are able to take this holographic blur and convert it into the sticks and stones and other familiar objects that make up our world. In other words, the smoothness of a piece of fine china and the feel of beach sand beneath our feet are really just elaborate versions of the phantom limb syndrome.

—Michael Talbot
The Amazing Holographic Universe

From a Newtonian viewpoint the universe can be likened to a machine but from a quantum viewpoint the universe is consciousness—thinking, creating, conceiving.

The universe begins to look more like a great thought than like a great machine.

—Sir James Jeans
British Astronomer

Reality is constructed out of information, not bits of matter.

Physicists are entertaining the possibility that reality might be literally constructed out of information. From a quantum perspective, the universe appears to be made out of bits of information rather than bits of matter or energy. Wheeler proposed that we live in a participatory universe in which we—by our act of asking questions of Nature—participate in the creation of the observed world.

—Dean Radin
Entangled Minds

In the quantum universe there is no past, no present, no future—and *no death*.

Quantum waves do travel in both directions through time. Therefore, in the fullest sense of the word, existence becomes a sum of all information. Like a great sea with far-reaching shores. It's a place where all possibilities exist simultaneously. There is no past, no present, and no future,—there just is.

—Joseph McMoneagle
Mind Trek

Reality is a matter of how we put together the bits and bytes.

It from bit

—John Archibald Wheeler
Physicist

Like energy, consciousness cannot be destroyed, it can only be transformed.

The persistence of gravity, like the persistence of light, points to the enduring if not eternal nature of information and energy. To the extent that consciousness is a fundamental property of an interconnected feedback universe, like energy itself, it cannot be destroyed but only can be transformed.... The "soul" and "spirit" of a living person will continue after bodily death as a "living info-energy system" in the vacuum of space.

—Gary E. Schwartz
The Afterlife Experiments

If consciousness continues after we die, then it is easier to understand what the mystics mean when they say that life is but a dream. We live; we die; we awaken from the dream . . . and then?

LIFE IS BUT A DREAM

Children yet, the tale to hear,
Eager eye and willing ear,
Lovingly shall nestle near.

In a Wonderland they lie,
Dreaming as the days go by,
Dreaming as the summers die.

Ever drifting down the stream—
Lingering in the golden gleam—
Life, what is it but a dream?

-Lewis Carroll
Through the Looking Glass

THERE IS NO DEATH

There is no death! The stars go down
To rise upon some other shore,
And bright in heaven's jewelled crown
They shine forever more.

There is no death! The forest leaves
Convert to life the viewless air;
The rocks disorganize to feed
The hungry moss they bear.

There is no death! The dust we tread
Shall change, beneath the summer showers,
To golden grain, or mellow fruit,
Or rainbow-tinted flowers.

There is no death! The leaves may fall.
The flowers may fade and pass away—
They only wait, through wintry hours,
The warm sweet breath of May.

There is no death! The choicest gifts
That heaven hath kindly lent to earth
Are ever first to seek again
The country of their birth.

And all things that for growth of joy
Are worthy of our love or care,
Whose loss has left us desolate,
Are safely garnered there.

Though life become a dreary waste,
We know its fairest, sweetest flowers,
Transplanted into paradise,
Adorn immortal bowers.

The voice of bird-like melody
That we have missed and mourned so long
Now mingles with the angel choir
In everlasting song.

There is no death! Although we grieve
When beautiful, familiar forms
That we have learned to love are torn
From our embracing arms;

Although with bowed and breaking heart,
With sable garb and silent tread,
We bear their senseless dust to rest,
And say that they are "dead."

They are not dead! They have but passed
Beyond the mists that blind us here
Into the new and larger life
Of that serener sphere.

They have but dropped their robe of clay
To put their shining raiment on;
They have not wandered far away—
They are not "lost" or "gone."

Though disenthralled and glorified,
They still are here and love us yet;
The dear ones they have left behind
They never can forget.

And sometimes, when our hearts grow faint
Amid temptations fierce and deep,
Or when the wildly raging waves
Of grief or passion sweep,

We feel upon our fevered brow
Their gentle touch, their breath of balm;
Their arms enfold us,
And our hearts grow comforted and calm.

And ever near us, though unseen,
The dear, immortal spirits tread;
For all the boundless universe is life—
There are no dead.

—James L. M'Creery

the challenge of death

D eath challenges us to find the meaning of life, and with it, genuine happiness. It is nature's way of goading us to discover our true condition, our real self—beyond the transience and ephemerality of this material world. And not only this world, but all worlds.

—John W. White
A Practical Guide to Death and Dying

If there is an Afterlife, what will it be like?

If our unique consciousness continues after we die so that we become a kind of mind without a body, so that we are still the individuals we were in life, then we remain in essence who we are with all of our foibles.

Our work is not over just because our life is over, just because we happen to die.

The problems and issues, hang-up and obsessions that we develop and cultivate during life are not likely to disappear miraculously upon death, because they are a part of who we are. What we do not deal with during life, we will have to deal with after life.

—Timothy Owe
Beyond Death

Consciousness is the fundamental force that creates and sustains the universe, not energy or matter.

Mind can influence matter. If consciousness were merely an illusion it would not be able to influence the physical world.

Consciousness has non-local qualities that physical world lacks.

What we do not deal with during life, we will have to deal with after life. If our consciousness is an eternal force that we are ultimately in charge of, then sooner or later we will have to deal with whatever we make of our minds. What we make of life, we will also make of death.

—Timothy Owe
Beyond Death

The problems and issues and hang-ups and obsessions that we develop and cultivate during life are not likely to disappear miraculously upon death, because they are part of who we are.

We exist in a universe of our own *interpretation.* In a reality of our consciousness we must relate to everything through the nature of our own consciousness.

—Timothy Owe
Beyond Death

FOUR POSSIBILITIES

It may be that what happens after death is what we expect to happen. Without a body we are simply mind—pure consciousness. So we may be able to create any after death reality. It may all depend on our pre-conceptions.

When remote viewer Lyn Buchanan told his training officer that he couldn't access people who were dying, his trainer gave him targets of dying people for several dozen sessions. After accessing the target person, the monitor would move Buchanan up to and through the moment of death. Buchanan says that targets went to one of four places on the "other side"—Heaven, Hell, Oblivion or Reincarnation.

Heaven

The dying person ended up in a place that had all of the physical attributes of our world, except that everything was "perfect" and there was an ambience of absolute and wonderful bliss.

Hell

On the other side of the death experience the person wound up in a glowing blackness with a dull and sinister orange glow and a feeling of total and complete horror.

Oblivion

The third place was no place at all. When Buchanan follow the person through the death experience there would suddenly be no person at all—they just stopped existing.

Reincarnation

The fourth possibility was reincarnating into another life. The dying person would suddenly have other physical characteristics, different surroundings, different life situations. Interestingly, they were not reborn as a baby but suddenly became a child of around twelve or thirteen years old.

Anyone who says that there is no afterlife might be just as correct as the person who says there is. The person who says that there is only one life on Earth may be just as correct as the person who says that we are reincarnated hundreds or thousands of times before moving on. The person who says there is no Heaven or Hell may be just as correct as the person who says that those places do exist.

—Lyn Buchanan
The Seventh Sense

WHAT HAPPENS AFTER DEATH?

Seeker: What happens after death, Shaman Woman?

Shaman: Why ask me?

Seeker: Because you're a shaman.

Shaman: Yes, that is so. But I am not a *dead* shaman.

14

EXPERTS QUOTED

Allen, Woody. (1935-) American film director, writer, comedian, playwright.

Altea, Rosemary. (1946-) Author and psychic. [rosemaryaltea.com]

Anderson, George. Medium, author. [georgeanderson.com]

Asimov, Isaac. (1920-1992) Russian-born science fiction writer.

Atwater, P.M.H. (1937-) Intuitive counselor and visionary author known for her research on the Near-Death Experience, [cinemind.com/atwater]

Bacon, Francis. (1561-1626) English philosopher, statesman and author. Catalyst of the scientific revolution.

Barrett, Sir William. (1844-1925) English physicist, co-founder of the Society for Psychical Research.

Bateson, Gregory. (1904-1980) British anthropologist, linquist.

Berry, Sheila M. RN Nurse.

Besan, Annie. Author, spiritualist of late 19th century.

Bierce, Ambrose. (1842-1914) American editorialist, journalist, writer and satirist.

Blake, William. (1757-1827) English romantic poet.

Blind, Mathilde. (1841-1896) Victorian woman poet.

Bodine, Echo. Medium and author. [echobodine.com]

Bohn, David. (1917-1994) Foremost theoretical physicist.

Bookbinder, David J. (1951-) Photographer, manadala artist.

Browne, Sir Thomas. (1605-1682) English author.

Buchanan, Lyn. Author, former member of US military remote viewing unit.[crviewer.com]

Butler, Samuel. (1835-1902) Iconoclastic Victorian author.

Cannon, Dolores. Psychic researcher and regressionist. Expert on the prophecies of Nostradamus. [ozakmt.com/cannon.htm]

Carroll, Lewis. Pen name for Charles Lutwidge Dodgson, author of *Alice in Wonderland* series.

Cayce, Edgar. (1877-1945) The sleeping psychic. [edgarcayce.org]

Chopra, Deepak. (1946-) Indian MD, spiritual author. [chopra.com]

Christ, Jesus. (1-36) Central figure of Christianity; believed to be incarnation of God.

Christopher, Stephen. Author.

Concetti, Rev. Gino. Chief theological commentator for Vatican newspaper, *L'Osservatore Romano.*

Conrad, Joseph. (1857-1924) Polish novelist.

Dass, Ram. (1931-) Mystic formerly Dr. Richard Alpert fired from Harvard along with Timothy Leary for LSD misadventures.

Davies, Paul. (1946-) Physicists, writer, broadcaster.

Dawkins, Richard. (1941-) British ethologist, evolutionary biologist and popular science writer.

de Lint, Charles. (1951-) Canadian fantasy writer, pseudonym Samuel M. Key.

Descartes, Rene. (1596-1650) French philosopher.

Dietrich, Marlene. (1901-1992) German-born American actress.

Donne, John. (1572-1631) Metaphysical poet and preacher.

Dyer, Dr. Wayne W. (1940-) Counselor educator, popular spiritual self-help author. [drwaynedyer.com]

Eagle, White. Shaman, author.

Ecclesiastes. Book of the Hebrew Bible. Old Testament.

Edwards, Harry. (1893-1976) Medium, spiritual healer.

Ellis, Alice Thomas. (1932-2005) British author and editor.

Epicurus. (341-270 BC) Ancient Greek philosopher and founder of Epicureanism.

Euripides. (480 BC-406 BC) Ancient Greek playwright.

Faulkner, William. (1897-1962) American author. *As I Lay Dying.*

Fenwick, MD, Dr. Peter. Neuropsychiatrist, King's College, London. Near-death experience researcher.

Fielding, Henry. (1707-1754) English novelist and dramatist.

Ford, Henry. (1863-1947) Founder of The Ford Motor Company, developed the assembly line and mass production.

Frederick the Great. (1712-1786) Frederick II, King of Prussia.

Fuller, R. Buckminster. (1895-1983) American architect, author, futurist and visionary.

Galilei, Galileo. (1564-1642) Italian physicist, mathematician, astronomer and philosopher. Father of science.

Gates, Bill. (1955-) Founder of Microsoft, American business magnate and philanthropist

Geis, R. Author.

Ghandi, Mahatma. (1869-1948) Major political and spiritual leader of India.

Gibran, Kahlil. (1883-1931) Lebanese artist, poet, writer, philosopher and theologian.

Giovetti, Paola. Hindu scholar, author.

Goff, Rory. Spiritual writer. [rorygoff.com]

Goudey, R.F. Reincarnation author.

Govinda, Lama Anagarika. (1898-1985) Expositor of Tibetan Buddhism.

Graham, Dr. Billy. (1918-) Evangelist minister.

Grof, M.D., Stanislav. (1931-) Czech psychologist; founder of transpersonal psychology; researcher of altered states. [stanislavgrof.com]

Guggenheim, Bill & Judy. Authors; researchers into after-death communication and visitations. [after-death.com]

Gurdjieff, George. (1866-1949) Armenian mystic and spiritual teacher.

Harman, Ph.D., Willis. (1918-1997) Futurist, author, social scientist with SRI International; President of Noetic Sciences.

Harris, Robert Alton. (1953-1992) Career criminal and executed murderer.

Harrison, George. (1943-2001) English rock guitarist in The Beatles.

Hawthorne, Nathaniel. (1804-1864) American novelist and short-story writer.

Helprin, Mark. (1947-) American short-story writer.

Hesse, Hermann. (1877-1962) German-Swiss poet, novelist, painter; 1946 Nobel Prize in literature.

Hood, Thomas. (1799-1845) British humorist and poet.

Horton, Doug. Author.

Hyslop, James. (1854-1920) Psychologist and psychical researcher; Professor of Logic at Columbia University.

James, William. (1842-1910) American psychologist and philosopher; author in pragmatism.

Jeans, Sir James. (1877-1946) English physicist, astronomer and mathematician.

Jung, Carl G. (1875-1961) Swiss psychiatrist and founder of analytical psychology, coined archetypes, the collective unconscious and synchronicity.

Keller, Helen. (1880-1968) First deaf-blind person to graduate from college; American author, activist and lecturer.

Klein, President. Author.

Kubler-Ross, Elisabeth. (1926-2004) Swiss-born psychiatrist specializing in death and dying, author

Leary, PhD. Timothy. (1920-1996). Psychologist, fugitive philosopher, Harvard professor fired for LSD antics.

Levine, Stephen. Poet, author, spiritual teacher, death counselor. [personaltransformation.com/Levine.html]

Lilly, M.D., John C. (1915-2001) Pioneer researcher into brain and consciousness, invented the isolation tank, studied dolphin communication and psychedelic drugs.

London, Jack. (1876-1916) American fiction author.

Longfellow, Henry Wadsworth. (1807-1882) American poet.

Lothian, Lori. Clairvoyant, astrologer, tarot reader. [accessnewage.com/tarology/LORI-BIO.HTM]

M'Creery, James L. 19th century poet.

Maeterlinck, Count Maurice. (1862-1949) Belgian poet, playwright. Winner of 1911 Nobel Prize in Literature.

Mailer, Norman. (1923-2007) American novelist.

Mann, Thomas. (1875-1955) German novelist; 1929 Nobel Prize in literature.

Margolis, Char. Psychic-intuitive, author. [char.net]

Maugham, William Somerset. (1874-1965) English playwright, novelist; best known for *Of Human Bondage.*

McCartney, Paul. (1942-) Musician and a member of The Beatles.

McCreery, John Luckey. (1835-1906) Poet.

McGraw, Dr. Phil. (1950-) American TV psychologist and author.

McMoneagle, Joseph. (1946-) Military Stargate remote viewer. [mceagle.com]

Mencken, H.L. (1880-1956) American journalist, essayist satirist.

Miller, Henry. (1981-1980) Controversial American writer and painter.

Mishlove, Ph.D., Jeffrey. Author; producer and host of the television series, Thinking Allowed, founder and president of the Intuition Network. [mishlove.com]

Mitchell, Edgar. (1930-) American pilot and astronaut.

Mitford, William. (1744-1827) English historian.

Moody, MD, Dr Raymond. (1944-) Author, psychologist, medical doctor. life after death researcher. [lifeafterlife.com]

Moyers, Bill. (1934-) American journalist and public commentator.

Nickell, Joe. (1944-) Stage magician and skeptic.

Nietzsche, Friedrich. (1844-1900) German philosopher, philologist, existentialist, author.

Nobokov, Vladimir. (1899-1977) Russian-American novelists, author of *Lolita.*

Nostradamus. (1503-1566) French seer who made hundreds of prophecies.

Novak, Peter. Author who combines modern science and ancient scripture.

Osis, Dr. Karlis. (1917-1997) Psychologist and parapsychology researcher. American Society for Psychical Research.

Owe, Timothy. Consciousness author.

Parnia, M.D., Sam. UK researcher in life after death.

Poe, Edgar Allan. (1809-1849) American poet, short story writer of mystery and the macabre.

Pope Pius XII. (1876-1858) 260th Pope of Roman Catholic Church.

Pribram, Karl. (1919-) Neurosurgeon and theorist of cognition.

Priest, Nancy Woodbury. (1836-1870) Poet.

Puthoff, Ph.D., Harold. (1936-) SRI physicist, remote viewing researcher.

Radin, Dean. (1952-) Parapsychology researcher and author. [deanradin.com]

Renard, Pierre-Jules. (1864-1910) French author best known for *Les Histoires Naturelles*.

Riaikkenen, Roza. Consciousness author.

Ring, Ken. (1979-) Writes about near-death experiences.

Rinpoche, Tulku Thondop. Buddhist author.

Rooke, Andrew. Consciousness author.

Rossetti, Dante Gabriel. (1828-1882) English poet, illustrator, painter.

Rumi, Jelaluddin. (1207-1273) Persian poet and sufi philosopher.

Russek, PhD, Linda G., Consciousness researcher and author. [heartsciencefoundation.com]

Salinger, J.D. (1919-) American author best know for *The Catcher in the Rye*.

Sanders, George Henry. (1906-1972) Academy Award-winning English film and television actor.

Sartori RGN, PhD, Dr. Penny. Senior Intensive Care Nurse, Morriston Hospital in Swansea

Satchidananda, Swami. (1914-2002) Indian religious figure, spiritual teacher and yoga adept.

Schopenhauer, Arthur. (1788-1860) German philosopher.

Schrodinger, Erwin. (1887-1961) Nobel Physicist famous for contributions to quantum mechanics and *Schrodinger's Cat.*

Schwartz, Stephan A. Consciousness author. [stephanaschwartz.com]

Schwartz, Gary E. Professor of psychology University of Arizona, author and researcher in afterlife. [drgaryschwartz.com]

Scott, Sir Walter. (1771-1832) Scottish writer, poet, historical novelist.

Scott-Holland, Canon Henry. (1847-1918) Regius Professor of Divinity at University of Oxford; Canon of Christ Church, Oxford.

Seth. The third son of Adam and Eve, often channeled by seers.

Smith, Paul H. Author and military remote viewer. [rviewer.com]

Socrates. (469-399 BC) Classical Greek philosopher, founder of Western philosophy.

Steiger, Brad. (1936-) Writer and paranormal researcher. [bradandsherry.com]

Stevenson, MD, Ian. (1918-2007) Canadian psychiatrist, survival after death researcher.

Swann, Ingo. Author, co-creator of remote viewing and CIA Stargate Project.

Talbot, Michael. (1953-1992) Author writing on parallels between mysticism and quantum mechanics.

Targ, Russell. (1934-) SRI physicist, ESP researcher. [espresearcher.com]

Tattersall, Ian. Paleanthropologist, curator at American Museum of Natural History.

Theroux, Paul. (1941-) American travel writer and novelist.

Thomas, Dylan. (1914-1953) Welsh poet.

Tolstoy, Count Leo. (1828-1910) Russian novelist, realist.

Traver, Amos. Author.

Van Dyke, Henry. (1852-1933) American author, educator, clergyman.

Van Praagh, James. (1958-) Medium and best selling author. [jamesvanpraagh.com]

Von Braun, Werner. (1912-1977) German rocket physicist and astronautics engineer.

Von Ward, Paul. Psychologist, protestant minister, writer and lecturer on consciousness and the soul. [vonward.com]

Wallace, James. Arizona death row inmate.

Walsch, Neale Donald. (1943-) American author of the *Conversations with God* series. [nealedonaldwalsch.com]

Warhol, Andy. (1928-1987) American artist.

Washington, George. (1732-1799) First President of the United States.

Watts, Alan W. (1915-1973) Philosopher, writer, interpreter of Asian philosophies for Western audience.

Weinstein, Howard. (1954-) Science fiction writer.

Weiss, MD, Brian. Psychiatrist, past-life regression specialist. [brianweiss.com]

Wheeler, John Archibald. (1911-2008) American theoretical physicist; coined "black hole", "worm hole" and "it from bit".

White, John W. Author on death and dying.

Wills-Brandon, Carla. Author, deathbed researcher. [carlawillsbrandon.com]

Winslow, Jacques-Benigne. (1669-1760) Danish anatomist.

Wolf, Fred Alan. "Dr. Quantum" (1934-) Theoretical physicist, author on subjects of quantum physics, consciousness, and their relationship. [fredalanwolf.com].

Wollstonecraft, Mary. (1759-1797) Early American feminist, author of *A Vindication of the Rights of Women.*

Zammit, Victor. Australian author and paranormal research. [victorzammit.com]

Zukav, Gary. Best selling author who combines spirituality and quantum physics. [zukav.com]

15

SUGGESTED READING

Altea, Rosemary, *The Eagle and The Rose*, Warner Vision Books, 1995.

Altea, Rosemary, *Proud Spirit Lessons, Insights & Healing from "The Voice of the Spirit World"*, Eagle Book William Morrow, 1997.

Anderson, George, *George Anderson's Lessons from the Light: Extraordinary Messages of Comfort and Hope from the Other Side,* Berkley Trade, 2000.

Atwater. P.M.H., *The Big Book of Near Death Experiences: The Ultimate Guide to What Happens When We Die*, Hampton Roads, 2007.

Atwater. P.M.H., *Coming Back To Life: Examining the After-Effects of the Near-Death Experience,* Transpersonal Publishing, 2008.

Atwater. P.M.H., *We Live Forever: The Real Truth About Death*, A.R.E. Press, 2004.

Bodine, Echo, *Echoes of the Soul: Moving Beyond the Light,* New World Library, 1999.

Bodine, Echo, *Relax, It's Only a Ghost: My Adventures with Spirits, Hauntings and Things That Go Bump in the Night,* Fair Winds Press, 2001.

Bohn, David, *The Undivided Universe*, Routledge, 1995.

Browne, Silvia, *God, Creation, and Tools for Life*, Hay House, 2000.

Buchanan, Lyn, *The Seventh Sense: Secrets of Remote Viewing As Told by a "Psychic Spy" for the U.S. Military*, Paraview Pocket Books, 2003.

Cannon, Dolores, *Between Death & Life: Conversations with a Spirit,* Zark Mountain Publishers, 1993.

Chopra, Deepak, *Life After Death: The Burden of Proof,* Harmony Books, 2006.

Dalzell, L.C.S.W., George E., *Messages: Evidence for Life After Death,* Hampton Roads, 1988, 1991.

Edward, John, *Crossing Over: The Stories Behind the Stories,* Jodere Group, 2001.

Edward, John, *One Last Time: A Psychic Medium Speaks to Those We Have Loved and Lost,* Berkley Books, 1988.

Grof, MD, Stanislav, *The Holotropic Mind,* HarperOne, 1993.

Guggenheim, Bill and Judy, *Hello From Heaven! A New Field of Research—After-Death Communication—Confirms That Life and Love Are Eternal,* Bantam Books, 1995.

Keller, Timothy, *The Reason for God: Belief in an Age of Skepticism,* Dutton Books, 2008.

Kubler-Ross, Elisabeth, *On Life After Death,* Celestial Arts, 1991.

LaGrand, Louis E., *After Death Communication: Final Farewells,* Llewellyn Publications, 1997.

Lilly, MD, John C., *The Scientist: A Metaphysical Autobiography,* Ronin Publishing, 1996.

Margolis, Char, *Questions from Earth, Answers from Haven: A Psychic Intuitive's Discussion of Life, Death, and What Awaits Us Beyond,* St. Martin's Press, 1999.

Martin, Joel and Patricia Romanowski, *We Are Not Forgotten: George Anderson's Messages of Love and Hope from the Other Side,* Berkley Books, 1991.

Martin, Joel and Patricia Romanowski, *We Don't Die: George Anderson's Conversations with the Other Side,* Berkley Books, 1988.

Meek, George, W., *After We Die, What Then? Evidence You Will Love Forever,* Ariel Press, 1987.

McMoneagle, Joseph, *Mind Trek: Exploring Consciousness, Time, and Space Through Remote Viewing,* Hampton Roads, 1997.

Mishlove, PhD, Jeffrey, *The Roots of Consciousness: The Classic Encyclopedia of Consciousness Studies Revised and Expanded,* Marlowe & Co., 1997.

Moody, Jr., MD, Raymond A., *Life After Life: The Investigation of a Phenomenon—Survival of Bodily Death,* Bantam Books, 1975.

Moody, Jr., MD, Raymond A., *The Light Beyond: New Explorations of Life After Life,* Bantam Books, 1988.

Moody, Jr., MD, Raymond A., *Reunions: Visionary Encounters With Departed Loved Ones,* Ivy Books, 1994.

Monroe, Robert A., *Journeys Out of the Body,* Doubleday Anchor 1971.

Morehouse, David, *The Psychic Warrior: The True Story of America's Foremost Psychic Spy and the Cover-Up of the CIA's Top-Secret Stargate Program,* St. Martin's Paperbacks, 1996.

Owe, Timothy, *Beyond Death: Empirical Evidence of the Human Soul,* New Falcon Publications, 2003.

Peterson, Robert, *Out of Body Experiences: How to Have Them and What to Expect,* Hampton Roads, 1997.

Radin, Dean, *Entangled Minds: Extrasensory Experiences in a Quantum Reality*, Paraview Pocket Books, 2006.

Riaikkenen, Roza and Andrew Rooke, Beyond Caterpillar Consciousness, *Sunrise Mag.*, Aug/Sep 2006.

Ring, Ken, *Lessons from the Light: What We Can Learn from the Near-Death Experience*, Moment Point Press, 2006.

Schlotterbeck, Karl, *Living Your Past Lives: The Psychology of Past-Life Regression*, Ballantine Books, 1987.

Schwartz, PhD, Gary E., *The Afterlife Experiments: Breakthrough Scientific Evidence of Life After Death*, Pocket Books, 2002.

Schwartz, PhD, Gary E., *The G.O.D. Experiments: How Science is Discovering God in Everything Including Us*, Atria Books, 2006.

Schwartz, PhD, Gary E. and Linda G.S. Russek, *The Living Energy Universe*, Hampton Roads, 2006.

Schwartz, Stephen A., *Opening To The Infinite*, Nemoseen Media, 2007.

Sheldrake, Rupert, *Dogs That Know When Their Owners Are Coming Home: And Other Unexplained Powers of Animals*, Three Rivers Press, 2000.

Sheldrake, Rupert, *The Sense of Being Stared At: And Other Unexplained Powers of the Human Mind*, Three Rivers Press, 2004.

Smith, Paul H., *Reading the Enemy's Mind: Inside Star Gate—America's Psychic Espionage Program*, Tom Doherty Books, 2005.

Smith, Suzy, Gary E. R. Schwartz, and Linda G.S. Russek, *The Afterlife Codes: Searching for Evidence of the Survival of the Soul*, Hampton Roads Publishing, 2000.

Talbot, Michael, *The Amazing Holographic Universe*, Harper Perennial, 1992.

Targ, Russell, *Limitless Mind: A Guide to Remote Viewing and Transformation of Consciousness*, New World Library, 2004.

Targ, Russell, and Harold E. Puthoff, *Mind-Reach: Scientists Look at Psychic Abilities*, Hampton Roads, 2005.

Thurman, Robert, Translator, *The Tibetan Book of the Dead: The Great Book of Natural Liberation Through Understanding in the Between*, Bantam, 1993.

Van Praagh, James, *Reaching to Heaven: A Spiritual Journey Through Life and Death*, Dutton Books, 1999.

Van Praagh, James, *Talking to Heaven: A Medium's Message of Life After Death*, Dutton Book, 1997.

Von Ward, Paul, *The Soul Genome: Science and Reincarnation*, Fenestra Books, 2008.

Walsch, Neale Donald, *Conversations with God: An Uncommon Dialogue*, Book 1, G. P. Putnam's Sons, 1995.

Watts, Alan W., *The Book: On the Taboo Against Knowing Who You Are*, Colliar Books, 1966.

Weiss, MD, Brian, L., *Many Lives, Many Masters: The True Story of a Prominent Psychiatrist, His Young Patient, and he Past-Life Therapy That Changed Both Their Lives*, Fireside Books, 1988.

Weiss, MD, Brian, L., *Only Love is Real: A Story of Soulmates Reunited*, Warner Books, 1996.

Weiss, MD, Brian, L., *Through Time into Healing: Discovering the Power of Regression Therapy to Erase Trauma and Transform Minds, Body, and Relationships*, Fireside Book, 1992.

White, John W., *A Practical Guide to Death and Dying*, Paraview Special Ed., 2004.

Wills-Brandon, Carla, *One Last Hug Before I Go: The Mystery and Meaning of Deathbed Visions*, HCI, 2000.

Wolf, Fred Alan, *Taking the Quantum Leap: The New Physics for Nonscientists*, Harper Perennial, 1989.

Wolf, Fred Alan, *Mind into Matter: A New Alchemy of Science and Spirit*, Moment Point Press, 2000.

Wolf, Fred Alan, *The Spiritual Universe: One Physicists Vision of Spirit, Soul, Matter, and Self*, Moment Point Press, 1998.

Wolf, Fred Alan, *Parallel Universes*, Simon & Schuster, 1990.

Zukav, Gary, *The Seat of the Soul*, A Fireside Book, 1989.

Zukav, Gary, *Dancing Wu Li Masters: An Overview of the New Physics*, HarperOne, 2001.